Michael Oakeshott, The Ancient Greeks,
and the Philosophical Study of Politics

British Idealist Studies Series 1: Oakeshott

imprint-academic.com/idealists

Michael Oakeshott, The Ancient Greeks, and the Philosophical Study of Politics

Eric Steven Kos

imprint-academic.com

Published in the UK by Imprint Academic
PO Box 200, Exeter EX5 5YX, UK

Published in the USA by Imprint Academic
Philosophy Documentation Center
PO Box 7147, Charlottesville, VA 22906-7147, USA

ISBN 9 781845 400750

A CIP catalogue record for this book is available from the
British Library and US Library of Congress

imprint-academic.com/idealists

Unless we know what philosophy is, unless we have a clear conception of its aims and results, the history of philosophy must remain a blank, a sealed book, a mere repertory of dead and unprofitable dogmas.

James Frederick Ferrier
Lectures on Greek Philosophy (1866, I:1).

Contents

Acknowledgements

It is perhaps odd to acknowledge a debt to the object of one's research, though if the focus is remarkable human beings, it is perhaps more understandable. Michael Oakeshott is one such remarkable individual, not least for his generosity. His elegant prose invited me in and his unostentatious erudition and insight made me stay. I had the good fortune to visit him on the Dorset coast in the spring of 1990. I was regretfully too young to appreciate the full opportunity presented. Nevertheless I was warmly met and treated to the patient, thoughtful conversation and delicious soup for which he has come to be known. I doubt I could have done better in having Oakeshott as a touchstone for my thought and work.

I have been surrounded by excellent individuals throughout this particular project. This revised version of my Ph.D. thesis at the University of Michigan would not have been possible without the help and critical feedback of Arlene W. Saxonhouse, Edwin M. Curley, Mika T. LaVaque-Manty, and Timothy Fuller. Arlene Saxonhouse was a model mentor, both as editor and in providing a fantastic apprenticeship to her own research and writing. Timothy Fuller's inspiration and critical encouragement predates even my acquaintance with Oakeshott's work.

I would not have been able to do the initial research without the financial support of the Earhart Foundation, which allowed me to work on the Oakeshott archives at the London School of Economics and Political Science in the fall of 2001.

I have benefited from numerous discussions with colleagues and mentors throughout this process, chief among them are Arlene W. Saxonhouse, Kimberly K. Smith, Edward Clayton, and Todd Breyfogle, the latter of whom initially introduced me to the work of Michael Oakeshott. Early feedback from the lively and thoughtful participants in the

Michael Oakeshott Association was also invaluable. I cannot begin to measure the significance of the conversations I have had with these individuals. My thanks also go to Noël K. O'Sullivan and Keith Sutherland at Imprint Academic. I benefited greatly from their professionalism and concise and thoughtful advice.

Finally, I owe a debt too great to measure for the love and support of my wonderful family. They have sacrificed and lent encouragement at critical times along the way. My wife Shannon especially deserves note. She not only provided technical assistance throughout the writing, but her persistent encouragement and love have been, and continue to be, a wellspring that sustains me.

Abbreviations

CL   'A Philosophical Approach to Politics: My First Course of Lectures', LSE File 1/1/7

CPJ   'The Concept of a Philosophical Jurisprudence', *Politica*, 3:203–22, 345–60

EGP   Notebook titled 'Early Greek Philosophy', LSE File 2/4/1

EM   *Experience and Its Modes* (Cambridge University Press, 1933)

LSE   *Lectures in the History of Political Thought* (Imprint Academic, 2006)

MPME   *Morality and Politics in Modern Europe* (Yale University Press, 1993)

OHC   *On Human Conduct* (Clarendon Press, 1975)

Rep I, II   Notebooks on the *Republic*, LSE Files 2/2/1–2

RIP   *Rationalism in Politics* (Liberty Fund, 1991)

RPML   *Religion, Politics and the Moral Life* (Yale University Press, 1993)

VLL   *The Voice of Liberal Learning* (Yale University Press, 1989)

Chapter I

Oakeshott and the Project in the Notebooks

Introduction

What exactly is it we are doing when we as teachers read and discuss with students some memorable work in the history of political thought? This has been an animating question for my thinking and this work. It is what initially drew me to the work of Michael Oakeshott, for it was a central concern of his as well. Oakeshott's unique response to the question 'What is political philosophy?' can help us puzzle through what would be a meaningful answer to this question. More particularly through an exploration of Oakeshott's confrontation with the beginnings of political philosophy, in the ancient Greeks, his unique vision of political philosophy emerges.[1] This conception of the character of political philosophy, though inspired by and deeply indebted to the ancient Greeks, is a distinctly modern view. It is a view that helps us work through the variety of meanings given to the term 'political theory' and to confront a series of contemporary challenges to the study of the history of political thought and to the study of 'great books'

---

[1]   The Greeks help us investigate this question of the character of political philosophy by returning us to the origins of this practice. From this perspective we can then assess the contemporary practice. One might of course, like Nietzsche, largely reject the practice as it comes to us from Plato, or one might embrace without modification the practice. More likely, one might selectively adopt characteristics of the original practice, as Oakeshott does. After the Nietzschean critique of Plato, many twentieth century political thinkers have only partly embraced the Platonic practice of philosophy. Zuckert (1996) has compiled a notable collection of theorists who only partially embraced Plato's formulation. One might also consider Arendt who more richly embraced the ancients and Karl Popper who did not. What is clear is that however one reacts to the early form of the practice of philosophy, as much (if not more) is revealed about the individual investigating the origins of philosophy as about the originators.

more generally. By considering how Oakeshott confronted the question of the origins of political philosophy, one can clarify the nature of the discipline and be better placed, as a result, to assess the character and value of the whole Western tradition of political thought.

The Value of the Notebooks

In his introduction to Hobbes's *Leviathan*, Oakeshott identified three broad traditions or patterns within the history of political thought. The supreme expression of these three traditions he found in three 'masterpieces' of political theory, which are respectively Plato's *Republic*, Hobbes's *Leviathan* and Hegel's *Philosophy of Right*. The first tradition, represented by Plato's *Republic*, has as its master-conceptions those of Reason and Nature. The second, represented by Hobbes' *Leviathan*, also "springs from the soil of Greece" and has as its master conceptions Will and Artifice. The third, which did not appear until the eighteenth century, is represented by Hegel's *Philosophy of Right*, and has as its master-conception the Rational Will (*RIP* 227–28). Although the influence of Hobbes and Hegel on Oakeshott's thought has been given substantial treatment in the critical literature, the influence of Plato has not been accorded similar treatment. A set of notebooks kept by Oakeshott, that have recently been made available for scholarship, helps to remedy this absence and to show why Oakeshott thought Plato's *Republic* was among the greatest works in the larger history of political thought.

The almost two dozen notebooks, used as primary sources for this project, are small notebooks written in Oakeshott's hand and used to record his thoughts on all kinds of different subjects throughout his life. A few are specifically dedicated to particular authors and particular works. There are lengthy notebooks on early Greek philosophers, on Plato's *Republic*, on Aristotle's *Ethics* and *Politics* and on Spinoza's writings. The early Greek philosophy notebook, the Plato notebooks and the Aristotle notebooks are the primary ones I have relied upon. These notebooks are mostly Oakeshott's own commentaries, but he also made extensive use of other commentaries and recorded passages from those works. He also made frequent cross-references to other notebooks and to other works he had read or was reading at the time.

One reason Plato's position in Oakeshott's thought is less clear than that of other philosophers who have influenced him is the qualified treatment Oakeshott himself gives to Plato in his published writings. In the instances Oakeshott endorses Plato's thinking, he inevitably offers a strong critique as well. The clearest example of this positive and then negative treatment of Plato is in Oakeshott's rendition of Plato's cave allegory in *On Human Conduct* (1975, 27–31), which I shall give a good deal of attention to below. The same criticism is not equally evident in Oakeshott's rather extensive scholarship on Hobbes or his brief treatments of Hegel.

The notebooks show the influence and importance Plato had for Oakeshott an influence only fleetingly glimpsed in the few references Oakeshott made to Plato in his published work. Searching for 'influences' is a precarious if not nefarious preoccupation. But, when the endeavor is not the marshalling authorities but an attempt to show what one theorist found of interest and relevance in another, the endeavor can be quite instructive. What can be gained by this search is a clearer understanding of what may be relevant in the history of political philosophy through a careful following of another's search for relevance. In the case of the ancient Greek thinkers, the character of political philosophy is thrown into sharper relief than it is with Hobbes or Hegel, both of whom, despite their differences, are modern and share more in common with Oakeshott and us. But, what could Oakeshott or we share with the ancient Greeks? They lived so long ago, how could their concerns have any meaningful relationship with Oakeshott's or ours? One persistent debate in contemporary political theory is over the continuing relevance of the Greeks. Oakeshott helps us assess the continuing relevance of ancient Greek political thought.

Oakeshott's confrontation with the ancient Greeks points out a number of central contributions that the ancient Greeks make to political philosophy. One of these contributions is to highlight a tradition of thought (animated by the conceptions of Reason and Nature) that remains a powerful line of philosophizing today. That is, Oakeshott highlights for us the dominant assumptions in ancient as well as current Platonism. As significant is the idealism Oakeshott finds in Plato (and Socrates), that Oakeshott sees as a source for avoiding the excesses of Platonism and the excesses of modern 'scientific' positivist and practical approaches to political philosophy.

Oakeshott's treatment of the ancient Greeks offers a rather powerful alternative to understanding the character of political philosophy over two dominant alternatives in Oakeshott's time and in ours. One commentator on Oakeshott understands Oakeshott's idealism as a response to two alternative philosophical understandings dominant in his time (Greenleaf 1966). The first he calls 'transcendental realism', and this alternative understands philosophy, following Plato, to aim at transcending the realm of becoming to enter the "realm of stable Being" where the universal essences that constitute reality reside (1966, 6). The second, 'empirical nominalism', holds that the only reality we can know is through our senses and reality is known through a method of scientific investigation pursued by natural science and physics (1966, 7). Hobbes, in some readings, might come to mind as a representative of this latter tradition.[2]

A more contemporary formulation of this philosophical dialectic is the debate between what might be called the 'Platonist school' of political philosophy and what has come to be called the Cambridge School of political philosophy. On the one hand there is an historicism that holds the only reasonably scientific and objective way to approach the history of political philosophy is to fill out the immediate historical context and show how a particular work is a response to that context. The alternative, we are urged, is to imagine a political philosopher answering questions that transcend time and space and revealing a reality that our normal, waking consciousness is only a pale reflection (a Platonic view). Oakeshott's rather eccentric treatment, particularly of Socrates but also of Plato, suggests a third approach: one that begins with an historical analysis but allows for the analysis of some texts within a much broader horizon.

The notebooks also help settle a significant debate among students of Oakeshott related to the question of how one reads the history of political thought. There has emerged a disagree-

---

[2]   In a rare moment, Oakeshott is critical of Hobbes for not having an adequate theory of volition (1937, 378) which reveals an inadequacy in this approach. Greenleaf's and Franco's (1990, 6) reading of Oakeshott is that like Rousseau (with his General Will), Hegel (with his Rational Will), Bradley (with his concrete universal) and Bosanquet (with his Real Will), he was trying to overcome the deficiencies of the two conflicting conceptions of philosophy. Oakeshott certainly saw this as one of the challenges of modern political thought as he indicates in what follows in his critique of Hobbes (1937, 378).

ment, made more explicit with the publication of Steven Gerencser's book *The Skeptic's Oakeshott* (2000), over the continuity of Oakeshott's thought over his lifetime. Gerencser's argument is that Oakeshott began, under the strong influence of Hegel and Bradley, as an 'absolute idealist' but then "leaves idealism behind" for a strongly skeptical position (2000, 20). A reply is that Oakeshott shifts his language to signal a mere change in emphasis and that it is impossible to show that Oakeshott's fundamentally idealist commitments ever changed over time (Coats 2000, 48–49). The 'substantial change' thesis rests, of course, on the premise that Oakeshott was a particular kind of idealist early on, and that from this early position a move was made to a position quite far way from the original one. The notebooks shed light on Oakeshott's original idealism. They reveal Oakeshott to be, if not a more skeptical and eccentric idealist early on, then at a minimum, not as firmly committed to the 'absolute idealism' that he is alleged to have had. What is at stake here is not merely clarification of what Oakeshott really meant, but a much larger question of the nature of the contribution Oakeshott may have made to political philosophy, and this point draws attention to another value of the notebooks, and that is the value of the idealism that Oakeshott embraced and propounded. Oakeshott himself was aware that calling himself an idealist was sufficient cause for some to reject anything he might have to say. "I am aware that in these days many readers will require no other evidence than this confession [of having an affinity with idealism] to condemn my view out of hand", Oakeshott says in his introduction to *Experience and Its Modes* (1933, 6). But his idealism is relevant precisely in helping us untangle and transcend the debates over the nature of philosophy mentioned earlier.

The notebooks also offer a more accessible iteration of Oakeshott's thinking. Oakeshott's understanding of philosophy sits at the center of his thinking,[3] and the value of his conception of philosophy to us can only be assessed if his central idea of philosophy is easily accessible. This analysis of the notebooks adds dimension to Oakeshott's conception of philosophy by showing how Oakeshott was a rather eccentric British Idealist. The way this eccentricity is established is by

---

[3]   Some of the earliest treatments of Oakeshott treated him predominantly as a theorist of political conservatism and not primarily, as he always self-identified, as a philosopher.

showing the central dilemmas Oakeshott struggled with in these the early Greek thinkers, in their metaphysical and epistemological positions, and in the refinement of philosophy occasioned by Socrates and Plato. How this eccentric position is played out is evident in Oakeshott's approach to the state and to the study of politics more generally. These two topics, the nature of the state and the nature of the study of politics in a university, allow for a clear exploration of what Oakeshott took from the Greeks, what he thought of use in the Greeks, and what he thought should be avoided to prevent modern iterations of ancient philosophical errors.

Beyond these important advantages, the notebooks also help us understand the value of the philosophical study of politics. As we shall see, Oakeshott imagines a rather large gap between the philosophical reflections on politics and practical reflections on politics. The philosophical study of politics comes after the practice of politics and is merely an attempt to explain and describe the practice itself. The question arises over the value of a philosophical treatment of politics if philosophy comes so late in the day to not be of practical value. Oakeshott has a rather unique response, though not an unfamiliar response to those who are acquainted with Socrates.

Philosophy, like art or Aristotelian friendship, is an end in itself for Oakeshott. In a reformulation of the Greek distinction between the private realm of necessity (*oikia*) and the public realm of freedom (*polis*) (reminiscent of Hannah Arendt's critique of the rise of the 'social' (1958)) Oakeshott is worried practical concerns might dominate if not extinguish other important human activities. The aim is to prevent life from becoming only work, the value of which is measured only in terms of the successful exploitation of the earth's resources; to avoid, as Oakeshott puts it in a memorable phrase, the 'deadliness of doing' (1995, 33).

Like the Bloomsbury group, Oakeshott is concerned to defend art and learning and their place in civilization and culture, but without succumbing to the impulse to position art and philosophy in such a way that it leads to snobbery or moral relativism.[4] In distinguishing practical thinking from philosophy, and these from science and art and history,

[4]   It is not exactly clear what relationship, if any, Oakeshott may have had with members of the Bloomsbury group. He did, however, write a revealing review of E.M. Forster's book *Two Cheers for Democracy*. What Oakeshott sees as bind-

Oakeshott resists the temptation to align these activities and explanatory modes in a progression or in a hierarchy. What results is the brilliant image of voices in conversation: an image that doesn't diminish the importance of each voice but by being conversational avoids any one voice dominating the discussion. The early genesis of this thought and image is found in the notebooks.

The Notebooks and Their Use

The notebooks pose methodological difficulties both in terms of the evidence they provide and in terms of how to approach them. How to deal with these notebooks as evidence is complex: imagine someone finding your own set of notes. There is a real difficulty in attempting to sort through why Oakeshott may have made a particular notation. Was a notation made because Oakeshott agreed with it, because it was meant to be a contrast or challenge to Oakeshott's view, was it meant to signal that a set of issues needed to be addressed in considering a particular topic, or was there some other reason for including it? The task is made more complicated in that Oakeshott drew heavily on a handful of secondary sources in each of his notebooks. Part of the job of the interpreter of the notebooks is to separate out what are Oakeshott's unprompted reflections on, say, Plato's *Republic,* versus those reflections inspired by say Bosanquet or Nettleship — two important secondary sources for Oakeshott. There is a further problem of determining whether Oakeshott was in fact endorsing some commentary by Bosanquet or Nettleship or again making a notation by way of contrast with his own view. There is a similar difficulty in dealing with cross-references to other works.

What I have endeavored to do throughout this investigation is to give a reason for each use of the notebook that is consistent with the immediate context and what I have taken to be the overall interpretation given in the notebook. Toward this end, I had to first distinguish Oakeshott's commentary from the commentary of other secondary sources, even though the two

---

ing together what otherwise is a miscellaneous collection of reflections is a "well-knit disposition". Forster is "the representative civilized man". But, unlike Montaigne, whom Forster invokes, Forster displays a "certain finicky self-centeredness" and reflects a temperament "touched with superiority" rather than true humility (1952, 436–38).

at times cannot be separated. I carefully read the secondary works and particularly the references and context of the references to sort out where Oakeshott was agreeing with the reading by the secondary source and where he may have been taking exception to the reading. The cross-references were also checked to try to understand the meaning –which at times seemed merely to signify a similar theme was touched upon, but at other times had rather significant implications for the interpretation of the notebooks. The references to other works Oakeshott was reading at the time were tracked down for their relevance.

A persistent attempt was made to compare what was written in the notebooks to what Oakeshott said in his published works. This latter method has its dangers. I have made every attempt not to 'read-back' into the notebooks fully developed thoughts Oakeshott worked out only much later in life. However, the later works are presumably attempts to answer questions that arose earlier. If the later, published works are answers, the answers can help illuminate the questions that arise in the earlier notebooks and so provide a useful entrée into the notebooks.

Cross-references to other notebooks also highlight a problem of how to structure my analysis of the notebooks. The cross-references signal a similar theme or themes that cut across all the notebooks, particularly the notebooks on specific authors (Plato, Aristotle, and Spinoza). One way to have proceeded could have been thematically. Another could have been to proceed chronologically beginning with Oakeshott's treatment of Thales and ending with Oakeshott's treatment of Plato. A third way could have been to work in chronological order of the notebooks themselves, in which case the Plato notebooks would be first followed by the earlier Greek thinkers. This was a difficult decision to make for each approach could be justified and each has some benefits.

That there is no clear way to proceed organizationally actually underscores a characteristic of Oakeshott's thought. Oakeshott thought holistically if not hermeneutically.[5] That is to say, Oakeshott never claimed, and often forcefully rejected, the idea that philosophy could be constructed on some partic-

---

[5]   See Nardin (2001) for an analysis of the connection of Oakeshott to a hermeneutic tradition and Gadamer.

ular foundation, either metaphysical or epistemological. Nevertheless, he was clearly interested in metaphysical and epistemological questions early in his life, and the themes of his first substantial work *Experience and Its Modes* (1933) and his interest and public acknowledgement of debt to F.H. Bradley and Hegel are clear indications of this interest. Like Socrates, Oakeshott sees a theory necessarily presupposing metaphysical and epistemological positions. If these positions are incoherent, the broader strength of the theory is diminished. But, he makes no claims that a theory can be built on these or any other foundation.

There might be a reason to proceed chronologically with the authors that Oakeshott investigates, but not because Oakeshott ever thought that the history of political thought is a history of continuing progress.[6] If the dates on the notebooks can be trusted, and there is no reason to not trust them, Oakeshott began with Plato dating his notebooks on the *Republic* July 1923, went on to investigate the earlier Greek thinkers (having dated his *Early Greek Philosophy* notebook in brackets October 1923), went on to investigate Aristotle's *Politics* and *Ethics* in 1924, and then returned to the early Greeks in October 1925 (which this notebook is also dated). Why did he do this? Did Plato and Aristotle fail to address some of the questions Oakeshott wanted addressed? Did Oakeshott think that to understand Plato and Aristotle that one needed to understand these earlier thinkers? Did he think that the pre-Socratics could only be understood by understanding the questions Plato and Aristotle were trying to answer?[7] It could be a combination of these reasons and others, but what is clear is that Oakeshott did go back and that what he found of interest in the pre-Socratics and in Socrates was a set of issues he found fundamental to philosophy, and that what interested him in these early thinkers became important topics he addressed in his earliest published work. I have then proceeded in chronological order of the authors addressed by the

---

[6]   Oakeshott explicitly eschews this belief. "I cannot detect a history of political thought which reveals a gradual accumulation of political wisdom and understanding", Oakeshott says in his first lecture in a course of lectures he gave at the London School of Economic in the 50s and 60s (*LSE* 32).

[7]   This was Gadamer's method in his lectures on the pre-Socratics, whom he thought would remain an enigma if not read as posing the questions Plato was trying to answer (1998, chapter 2).

notebooks. This is not to imply foundation; the order merely provided a nice progression from one set of issues to another.

The Structure of the Argument

Chapter 2

Chapter Two on the Presocratics sets forth the idealist framework for Oakeshott's ideas on philosophy and education. These early thinkers are of interest to Oakeshott because they grapple with and help us grapple with issues Oakeshott sees as central to the activity of philosophy. Oakeshott's focus is on the logical development of philosophy in these thinkers. The story is a familiar one of moving from myth or superstition to reason. And, then, a movement from an undifferentiated application of reason (a scientific approach generally) to a more narrow application of reason (philosophy). The movement is also one toward a more idealist perspective. That is, the logical development Oakeshott traces is one of a continuing refinement of a monistic conception of the cosmos and of philosophy as the search for a unity in the cosmos. The general movement Oakeshott sees in the Presocratics is the slow replacement of the search for a material unity with the search for a spiritual unity: a critical characteristic (at least since Hegel, if not earlier), of idealism.

The character of this spiritual unity is, interestingly, never adequately settled by Oakeshott in these notebooks. But, the character of that unity becomes the subject for investigation. The two theorists Parmenides and Herakleitos become important avenues through which Oakeshott explores the nature of this unity. However, the result is not to fix on some particular source of unity but as a way of winnowing down the variety of sources. That is to say, the notebooks reveal an Oakeshott committed to a monistic picture that he shares with other idealists, but also an Oakeshott whose thinking on the character of this unity is still an open question. The history of philosophy is a history of the process of slow refinement of this practice of philosophy.[8] Oakeshott's interest in the debates over idealism

---

[8]   In Oakeshott's first course of lectures, delivered at Cambridge in the Lenten terms of 1928 and 1929 (Franco 2004, 5), philosophy developed from undifferentiated curiosity and examination of everything to a rather particular exer-

and in the nature of philosophy would not necessarily be evident to those acquainted with Oakeshott as only a foe of Rationalism, though the critique of Rationalism is a part of this larger set of interests and concerns Oakeshott maintained throughout his life.

Chapter 3

Oakeshott's treatment of Socrates and the Sophists, the subject of Chapter Three, is noteworthy because it reveals a young Oakeshott who does not fit neatly into the mainstream of British Idealism for yet another reason. While Oakeshott shares the monism of other Idealists, an early, practical conservatism and profound skepticism is revealed in his reading of Socrates and in his replies both to the sensationalism of the Sophists and to their distinction between *physis* and *nomos*. British Idealists were, as a whole, reformers. Here, as we saw with the metaphysical questions in the second chapter, we find Oakeshott's attraction to Socrates' position on epistemological questions as a useful tonic to modern epistemological mistakes, without building a system on this epistemology. From as early as Cudworth's rebuke of Hobbes, a dominant concern of the Idealists has been to overcome the dualism between thought on the one side and sensation and desire on the other. For the idealists, will was not merely a product of desire or desire spurred on by unmediated experience. Reason, reflection, and thought were inextricably mixed with will and desire. One cannot will without willing something in particular. That something in particular is always influenced by the larger social context: a context consisting of a whole set of interwoven meanings. One might recognize this as a contribution from Hegel and why Oakeshott may have identified him with the tradition of the Rational Will in is introduction to *Leviathan*.

Oakeshott's reading of Socrates anticipates a large dose of the argument in *Experience and Its Modes* on sensationalism and shows the depth of the skepticism Oakeshott found in Socrates. It also sheds light on Oakeshott's conservatism. It is perhaps rather shocking that Oakeshott understands Socrates as a social conservative. Consistent with an emerging reading of

cise of one's critical faculties. These lectures are referred to as CI, followed by the lecture number and the page number.

Oakeshott, his conservatism was not the contemporary conservatism of the Tory party and Margaret Thatcher, or even the traditionalism of Burke, but a more deeply rooted conservatism of a philosopher: a skeptical and detached conservatism rooted in, he would say later on, a disposition toward the present rather than the past or a traditional doctrine and in a certain posture toward social change and innovation.[9] One of the few things a philosopher knows is that he/she knows not, and, though recognizing that one has commitments and needs commitments to engage in social change, one is pulled more powerfully toward trying to understand than toward action. He/she suspends those commitments in order to seek a better understanding.

Oakeshott's early interests were strongly reflected in his notebooks on the pre-Socratics and Socrates. He found in the pre-Socratics attempts to come to terms with the ever-changing multiplicity of what is observed by applying reason to overcome contradictions. The progress made by these pre-Socratics led to two different general approaches: the pluralism of the atomists and the monism first inspired by Thales and later pushed toward non-material causes by Pythagoras, Parmenides, Herakleitos, and Anaximander. The story of refinement is the story of the search for the unity amidst the multiplicity in a non-material, spiritual, or conceptual realm. In the conflict between the Sophists and Socrates we see Oakeshott's epistemological concerns closely linked to those of Socrates and to the metaphysical ideas he entertained with the pre-Socratics. If there was a unity of some sort, what is the nature of this unity and how can we come to know it? The unity that we are left with at the end of Oakeshott's investigation is a *unity of experience in thought*. This is the general philosophical position Oakeshott takes up and vigorously defends in his first major work *Experience and Its Modes*. As he says

> the view I propose to maintain is that experience is a single whole, within which modifications may be distinguished, but which admits of no final or absolute division; and that experience everywhere, not merely is inseparable from thought, but is itself a form of thought (*EM* 10).

The notebooks show just how early he was confronting this central issue of the value and ends of reflection. Does reflec-

---

[9]   See the essay 'On Being Conservative' (*RIP* 407–37).

tion yield a coherent unity or does it yield a disjointed multi-plicity or plurality? In confronting this question, Oakeshott helps us see not only the multiplicity and diversity of our thinking and acting, but also how this plurality all might be related as part of a larger whole and the character and source of this larger whole.

Chapter 4

Oakeshott's idealism is further worked out and connected to the activity of the philosopher in the Plato notebooks. In Chapter Four, Oakeshott's critical ambivalence toward Plato becomes clear. To put it succinctly, Oakeshott admired the skeptical idealism he inherited from Socrates but was critical of Plato's reforming zeal. An examination of this tension over Plato brings out Oakeshott's view of philosophy in stark detail. Through Oakeshott's rather peculiar reading of the *Republic* (I examine in particular Oakeshott's treatment of Cephalus and the Platonic Forms) we can see Oakeshott's view of where Plato made mistakes and where he was overly optimistic about the powers of philosophy. The critique of Plato goes beyond an early form of Oakeshott's latter critique of Rationalism. It is a powerful indictment of the Platonic aims of philosophy. However, it is not a complete indictment, for Oakeshott's treatment of Plato reads as a kind of struggle between Socrates and Plato, where Socrates ends up the more admirable philosopher. The particular version of philosophy that emerges from Oakeshott's treatment of Plato has powerful implications both in terms of understanding the state and in terms of the study of politics. The implications, in each of these areas, are explored in subsequent chapters.

Chapter 5

Oakeshott's treatment of Plato helps us to understand what is at stake in the metaphysical and epistemological concerns Oakeshott had early on. One of the central implications of the monism of Oakeshott and Plato is a shared (but not wholly shared) understanding of the relationship of the individual to the state. The state is the topic of Chapter Five. Oakeshott's approach to Plato and the state reveals the rather eccentric idealist position that Oakeshott is attempting to work out. The nature of Oakeshott's understanding of the monistic unity of experience is investigated and reveals a strong difference between Oakeshott and many other more contemporary idealists. One of the differences has to do with how spiritually this unity is understood. Oakeshott's Plato is decidedly non-mystical on this score. Further, this monism corrects, as Oakeshott sees it, some of the excesses of modern thinking on the relationship of the individual to the state (chiefly as expressed in social contract theorists). As we have seen, philosophical monism could be taken to imply a strong connection between theory and practice. Many idealists saw a strong connection; yet, Oakeshott does not. Oakeshott's critical ambivalence toward Plato on this score is instructive, for it shows not only Oakeshott's own understanding of philosophy as a more limited engagement but also the powerful influence Plato's understanding of the relationship between theory and practice has had on modern thinking. There is an interesting analogue in the way Oakeshott understands the nature of the modern European state and how he understands the tension in Plato between the philosophical impulse he gets from Socrates and his reforming impulse. The fact that Oakeshott and Plato understand the state as a reflection of the individuals who compose the state has powerful implications in terms of the study of politics. The study of politics, though narrowed by the concern with the nature of politics, involves a much broader study of culture and the understandings a particular people had of itself.

Chapter 6

The particular view of the state that Oakeshott and Plato share results in a shared interest in how to study politics. Both agree that the state is a reflection of the character of the individuals who make up the state, hence their shared interest in the character of the education appropriate to those individuals. It is, however, Oakeshott's divergence from Plato on the earlier discussed epistemological and philosophical grounds that has Oakeshott staking out an understanding of education and the study of politics quite different in consequence from the Plato of the *Republic*. This is the subject of Chapter Six. Oakeshott's criticism of Plato's understanding of the ends of education, as well as Oakeshott's reliance on Socrates more for his educational ideas, reveals Oakeshott's own unique view of an education radically severed from practical prescriptions.

Oakeshott's sharply non-practical, non-programmatic view of education provides us with a valuable approach to the study of politics. Oakeshott provides an approach to the study of politics (a discipline more susceptible than others to programs and practical advice) that helps defend a long tradition of reflection on politics from increasing contemporary demands to be practical - either state sponsored ones to increase math and science majors, or internal demands to politicize the classroom by introducing 'politics' into the classroom as a motivator of learning and good scholarship.[10]

Oakeshott's view of the philosophical study of politics also combines the strengths of two dominant understandings of the study of political philosophy: the historicist, or Cambridge School of political philosophy; and the 'timeless questions' school, an understanding of political philosophy and the history of political philosophy that is profoundly sensitive to historicity while engaging with others from the past in the investigation of perennial questions.

Chapter 7

Having, narrowed the practice of philosophy to a rather particular practice, what remains to discuss is its worth. The value of philosophy lies not, as it is for Plato, in its ability to clarify and reveal in order that we might better act. Rather, philosophy's value lies in its ability to explain, to remove some of the crookedness from our thinking. In this it is like other explanatory modes: like history, science, or a practical mode. Each is an attempt to explain our world and each carries with it certain assumptions about how to go about the business of explaining. The image Oakeshott uses to describe the relationship between these explanatory modes is as voices in conversation. What the image reflects is a view of each explanatory mode being valuable but different, one voice cannot substitute for another, and there is no hierarchy or a leader in a conversation.

---

[10] In its most recent iteration, the decision was made in the University of California system to rewrite its policy on offering political points of view in the classroom (Sexton 2003). This policy revision appears to be the impetus for the drive to provide 'intellectual diversity' on campuses through an Academic Bill of Rights, whereby all political views, however unpopular, cannot be discriminated against. See *The Chronicle of Higher Education* 50(23):A18–A19 for David Horowitz's proposed Rights and a debate between Horowitz and Stanley Fish in *The Chronicle Review* 2/13/04, p. B12–B14.

Philosophy is a voice among voices, and. like history, or pure science, or the poetic voice it is in danger of being dominated by the practical voice (which shouts most loudly today).

Philosophy, like poetry and history and science, when pursued for its own sake, helps prevent life from being a series of calculations about goals and goods, improving or conserving, good and bad, and success and failure. We must all engage in practical thinking and action in our everyday lives. But, human beings have developed activities that are more removed from these sorts of concerns, but no less valuable. Poetry, art, music, philosophy, science, the study of history, as they have emerged as practices today are equally valuable. They are, however, fundamentally altered when put in the service of some practical end. The great diversity of practices we have developed gets diminished by making all of our practices subservient to one single practice. Oakeshott's worry is that such a move diminishes the richness of life by turning it wholly into a struggle for power after power. These various activities need to be kept separate in order to maintain their worth and character and need to be accorded the dignity of equal voices in conversation.

Oakeshott and the Beginning of the Philosophic Quest

Oakeshott's engagement with the pre-Socratics results in an important story about the emergence of philosophy and a particular kind of progress that characterizes the history of philosophy. Through this highly abbreviated history of philosophy's beginnings we are able to see not only Oakeshott's rather curious position in the British Idealist tradition, but also have a window into how Oakeshott understands 'progress' in the history of philosophy. For Oakeshott, philosophic progress is measured in terms of logical progress. In fact, Oakeshott insists, all questions are logical before anything. The story of philosophy's genesis and development is not an unfamiliar one. The movement is one from myth or superstition to reason and is exemplified in Oakeshott's reading of the pre-Socratic poets. The poets reflect the necessary conditions for the emergence of philosophy: plurality, difference, conflict, and a skeptical attitude toward traditional accounts of meaning.

Philosophy begins when a rational unity is sought in the diversity of our experience, and Thales is taken as the first to advance on this quest. The quest is refined further in Oakeshott's reading of the pre-Socratic physiologists. The progress made by the physiologists, from Thales to Anaxagoras, is characterized as a logical progress toward a more idealist and away from a materialist perspective. Oakeshott indicates this is the nature of the progress on the title page of his "Early Greek Philosophy" notebook.[1] His

---

[1] This notebook is twenty-one pages in length and in Oakeshott's hand. The bulk of the notes and pagination with various quotations from other authors is

arrangement of these thinkers, he notes, is "in development, tho' not necessarily in chronology" (*EGP* 1). This raises an interesting point from the start. Oakeshott signals a difference between historical treatments and logical or philosophical treatments. To give a history of political thought is not necessarily to tell a story of inevitable historical progress. Rather, progress is measured logically. In fact, and this is an interesting theme that runs throughout Oakeshott's thinking, Oakeshott states in his first course of lectures[2] that "every question is logical before it can be historical" (*CL* II:1).

What constitutes logical progress, of course, becomes the question. Oakeshott sees this logical progress first as an attempt at finding a unity in our experience and as the disinterested search for what is real and true. That is, the progress is seen as a movement toward a monistic unity and a more universal explanation rather than a personal, subjective one. The progress is also seen as a shift to the search for a spiritual unity over a material unity. These points, of course, are distinguishing characteristics of all idealism—Platonic idealism, the idealism expressed in Cudworth's reply to Hobbes' alleged materialism,[3] Hegelian idealism, or the idealism of Bradley or McTaggart. What is sought here is a spiritual or idealist unity.

After the nature of the quest is refined, Oakeshott makes the character of this spiritual unity the central topic for investigation. Parmenides, Herakleitos, and Anaxagoras become central avenues through which Oakeshott investigates this question. The advance Oakeshott's identifies does not result in a perfectly defined picture of the nature of this unity, but achieves the more modest result of eliminating some of the possible sources of this unity. The character of 'progress' is measured in terms of being able to eliminate errors and advancing partial explanations in the search for a fuller and more comprehensive explanation.

The process of refinement mirrors how Oakeshott treats the history of philosophy in his first course of lectures. For the

---

on the recto page and explanatory notes are on the verso page. The explanatory notes refer to the adjacent page and so I shall make references to this work as EGP followed by the page number with a 'v' indicating the verso page of the adjacent page.

[2]   See Note 9 of Chapter 1.

[3]   A twentieth century British idealist identifies Cudworth (1617–1688) as the "real founder of British Idealism", though an idealist born out of due season as the next century would be dominated by empiricism (Muirhead 1992, 1,70).

early Greeks, philosophy was "equivalent to curiosity about anything and everything" and also as a set of opinions (*CL* I:4). And, despite Plato's (who was not available during much of the interim period) and Aristotle's (whose interests, if not his definition of philosophy, were rather wide) refinement, philosophy right down to the eighteenth century philosophy "means the undifferentiated pursuit of knowledge, 'curiosity' – what we now call, roughly, the 'scientific attitude'" (*CL* I:5). Oakeshott insists that the "tendency of history has been to distinguish intellectual pursuits from one another", that "Philosophy is something different from religion, different from Nat. Sci. It has its own character; it has individuality of its own" (*CL* I:6). *Experience and Its Modes* (1933) is a sustained explanation of the different types of explanatory modes or modes of experience that have been developed over time (practical, scientific, historical, philosophical), and their relationships. The distinct varieties of explanation and experience led Oakeshott to one of the images he is most recognized for, that each mode is a voice and these voices are related in conversation.[4]

The Genesis of Philosophy and Oakeshott's Treatment of the Pre-Socratics

Oakeshott's philosophical idealism is on display early (as much as a decade before his *Experience and its Modes* 1933) in his notebook on early Greek philosophy. The sources Oakeshott chose are decidedly idealist, if not always self-identified Hegelians.[5] Oakeshott drew heavily on James Frederick Ferrier's *Lectures on Greek Philosophy* (1866) and John Burnet's *Early Greek Philosophy* (1908) in the early portion of his *Early Greek Philosophy* notebook, particularly on the pre-Socratic physiologists. In the later portion of the notebook on the Sophists, Socrates, and the later schools, Oakeshott drew on Ferrier again and on Eduard Zeller's *A History of Greek*

---

[4] The most well known characterization comes in Oakeshott's essay *The Voice of Poetry in the Conversation of Mankind* (*RIP* 488–541). Here he adds the voice of poetry to the other modes he laid out in *Experience and Its Modes*. Indeed, the essay, Oakeshott says was undertaken to retract a hasty remark in *Experience and Its Modes*: most likely the remark that poetry is part of the practical mode.

[5] Oakeshott was studying at a time when idealism dominated the university, and in particular classical Greek studies. In the secondary literature one could not avoid idealist interpretations. It would only be later that the influence of G.E. Moore and A.J. Ayer would be felt in Greek studies.

Philosophy from the Earliest Period to the Time of Socrates (1881). Ferrier (1808–1864) was professor of moral philosophy and political economy at St. Andrews, and is credited with being "the pioneer" of the revival of idealism in Britain owing inspiration to Plato and Berkeley, rather than to Kant and to Hegel (Muirhead 1992, 14). Though Ferrier had read Hegel, he claimed not to have been influenced by him (Ferrier 1881, xxxviii). "I cannot follow what I do not understand" he is recorded to have said. And, he is alleged to have been seen reading Hegel upside down because he could not make sense of it right side up (Robbins 1982, 24).[6] John Burnet (1863–1928) studied classics at Edinburgh and Balliol (under D.G. Ritchie, a student of T.H. Green) and taught Greek at St. Andrews where he took an interest in Plato – an interest which became the source of his numerous publications on ancient Greek thinkers. Eduard Zeller (1814–1908) was a student and later teacher of philosophy and theology at University of Tübingen where he fell under the influence of Hegel. More significant than the sources Oakeshott used, however, is how he understands the contributions of the earliest Greek thinkers and for that we must turn to the notebooks.

Poets and the Necessary Context for Philosophy

For Oakeshott, philosophy emerged in ancient Greece when an old way of life gave way to a new one. Quoting Erdmann and Burnet, respectively, philosophy first appears when a customary way of life, supported by a mythical and superstitious set of beliefs, decays. "In order that not only laws and moral maxims, but also reflections on the totality of existence, and thus philosophy, may arise, the freshness of existence must die out still more, and decay must begin" (*EGP* 1; Erdmann 1890, 17).[7] "It was not till the primitive view of the world and the customary rules of life had broken down that the Greeks began

---

[6]   Ferrier wrote of Hegel in his *Institutes of Metaphysics* (1854) the following: "Whatever truth there may be in Hegel, it is certain his meaning cannot be wrung from him by any amount of mere reading, any more than the whiskey which is in bread–so at least we have been informed — can be extracted by squeezing the loaf into a tumbler" Quoted in Muirhead (1992, 154).

[7]   Johann Erdmann (1805–1892), Hegelian historian of philosophy who published a three volume history in German in 1878 which was translated into English in 1890, was originally a student of theology and later became professor of philosophy at Halle.

to feel the needs which philosophies of nature and of conduct seek to satisfy" (*EGP* 1; Burnet 1908, 1). Homer and Hesiod reflect this transitional period. Homer's reticence about the gods shows that the "old superstitions are going, men are ashamed of them, but do not cry out against them". Homer presents "light-hearted" and "joyful" tales about the gods (*EGP* 1).[8] The questioning of the previous view of the world has begun in Homer. Burnet says Homer disdains mentioning the older, savage tales, not out of ignorance but reticence (a point which Oakeshott records), though we find some of these tales in Hesiod (1908, 7).

Hesiod, in the *Theogony* in particular, reveals the "consciousness of change and decay" according to Oakeshott, and reflects a certain sadness and seriousness about this change (*EGP* 1). Oakeshott references section 27 of the *Theogony*. In this passage the daughters of Zeus speak to Hesiod saying "we know how to speak many false things as though they were true; but we know, when we will, to utter true things". Are these gods to be depended on then without question? Oakeshott makes a note that "it is time to tell the truth about the gods." Oakeshott is following Burnet's reading here who reads the *Theogony* as no mere revival of superstition and old tales about the gods. Rather, Burnet sees the "rudiments of what grew into Ionic science and history". He understands Hesiod's poems as doing more to "hasten the decay of the old ideas which he was seeking to arrest" by systematizing the stories of the gods. "System is necessarily fatal to so wayward a thing as mythology", Burnet notes (1908, 7).

It is in this questioning and dissatisfaction with previous tales about origins that gives impetus to philosophy according to Oakeshott. Oakeshott references Zeller on this point. "Traditional propriety of conduct had seccumbed before the spirit of innovation, because it rested upon instinct and custom, and not on any clear knowledge of its necessity. To be replaced on a permanent basis, propriety of conduct must rest upon knowledge" (1868, 34; *EGP* 1). This highlights an interesting ambigu-

---

[8]   Bruno Snell makes a similar point writing in the mid twentieth century. "Primitive man feels that he is bound to the gods; he has not yet roused himself to the awareness of his own freedom. The Greeks were the first to break through this barrier" and the early break is evident in Homer where the heroes of the *Iliad*, "no longer feel that they are the playthings of irrational forces" of magic and wizardry (1953, 31, 22).

ity in Oakeshott's thought – one that he was well aware of. On the one hand he self-identifies as having a conservative disposition, one that makes him skeptical of innovating on social practices. And, his critique of Rationalism suggests that persistent scrutiny of a practice (like learning or education) may have a distracting, if not corrosive, effect on the practice: formulating some premeditated ideal to be aimed at turns one's attention away from the actual practice and the kind of knowledge involved in engaging in the practice. Yet, philosophy aims at systematizing through rational scrutiny and can be quite radical and subversive of current understandings and practices in this quest. Perhaps this tension is more acute when custom and tradition cease to hold authority and there is a strong optimism about the exercise of reason. Under these conditions it may be difficult to know where to stop in scrutinizing social practices: one wants to *improve* upon social practice (we all recognize injustices), but we also wish to *enjoy* those practices which are available to us regardless of how ramshackle.

Oakeshott's lectures at London School of Economics on the Greeks delivered thirty years later in the 50s and 60s reflect a similar story about the rise of politics and philosophical reflection.[9] In the midst of early attempts by Achaean tribes to form more permanent unions there came the Doric invasions from the north around 1100 BC. These invasions savagely destroyed the nascent unions that had developed and the Greek world relapsed "into separate and often hostile tribal units" of mixed Achaean and Dorian influence (*LSE* 47–48). Tribal life was slowly replaced with new organizations.

> Upon these patriarchally governed tribes or village-households, whose unity was one of kinship, whose law was tribal custom, whose religion was a family religion, there supervened a new idiom of life: permanent unions of tribes (*LSE* 48).

Obscurely and slowly new religious and social communities emerged and the name given to this new form of organization was *polis* (*LSE* 49). Religion and political decision-making migrated out of the tribe/household (*oikia*) and into the public realm (*polis*) and "in doing so, had changed its character. The

---

[9] This is a remarkable set of thirty-three lectures that address many of the themes in Oakeshott's published writings and exemplify his approach to the history of political thought.

customs of the tribe were superseded by the law of the *polis*" (*LSE* 50–51). This change, no doubt, precipitated questioning as the old myths ceased to maintain the authority they once had.

One might recall the opening of the *Iliad*, where Homer implicitly questions the source of one's obligation to obey. Not only do Akhilleus (I:175)[10] and Thersites (II:257–278) directly question the political authority, but in reading or reciting this poem the question of the source of authority is raised. Sources are suggested and no resolution is put forth by Homer. Is it Agamemnon's sheer strength and divine right (I:91; I:300) or Akhilleus' greatness as a warrior that must be yielded to? Does Kalkhas' divine wisdom (I:79–85), Nestor's age and experience (I:298–300), or Odysseus' skill as a mariner and soldier and his understanding of the troops give him a right to rule? Homer's poem is riddled with uncertainty. This uncertainty permeates particular decisions, like whether to return to war or go back to one's private life or the decision to return Khryses' daughter. Uncertainty is also reflected in the conflicting understandings of authority, justice, and the heroic ethic. In one of the most memorable speeches in the poem, Akhilleus gropes for a redefinition of honor that meets his current predicament (IX:384–511).

These uncertainties called for a clarity previous explanations did not provide. "The problem of change and decay is always the one to move men to think", Oakeshott records Plato to have said (*EGP* 2). Early thinkers, Oakeshott notes, "had to turn their backs on the ruling conceptions which they had themselves inherited", "they gave up telling tales about the origin of things in order to look at things as they actually found them"(*EGP* 1). A rational search for a better explanation (philosophy) makes its appearance. Oakeshott, even in his critique of Rationalism much later in life, never abandoned reason, only narrowed its prerogative (as we shall see with Plato).

The philosophic turn began in questioning, confusion, and skepticism – a skepticism moved by the realization that a particular way of life was passing away. This would seem to be a critical juncture in the story of philosophy, for the conclusion could easily be reached (as later thinkers did) that all is flux; that there is no permanence. Oakeshott is not clear how the

---

[10] References are to book number followed by line number.

advance is made from the recognition of the problem of change and decay to the monistic principle of unity. The change in the history of philosophy is from a reliance on myths to a fundamental skepticism, to a "search for the original, fundamental, abiding substance, in the flux of things" (*EGP* 2). But the question remains why one would not stop with radical skepticism and the belief that things just change? Why seek a unity and permanence in all that 'seems' to change? Why suppose there is a unity in the first place?

Oakeshott does not fill out the story of how the movement is made, once myth is rejected, from questioning and skepticism to the search for unity.[11] Here, Oakeshott only suggests how the leap was made through the Greeks character and circumstances. Oakeshott is impressed with the Greeks' curiosity, their "desire to experience and discover" that enabled them to gain knowledge, their "daring of speculation", that they were "great observers of facts" and "did not deceive themselves with stories" (*EGP* 2). In Oakeshott's LSE lectures of the 50s and 60s, he notes how different sets of characteristics the Greeks possessed became embodied in a legend about Achaean and Dorian strains embedded in the Greek character. "The Achaean element was believed to supply the restlessness, the instability, and the curiosity of the Greek character; its easy fascination with what was new and its delight in change, its sense of humor. The Dorian element was believed to supply the dour more severe and disciplined, and conservative element" (*LSE* 48). The Greek character, then, could be an explanation: rational curiosity perhaps presumes a rational world of some kind.

Oakeshott also remarks that in the face of change there was "one comfort—Reality cannot perish" (*EGP* 2). Perhaps the thought that there was something more than flux was psychologically reassuring and a consolation to a people facing change, much like the Stoic and Epicurean doctrines provided a comforting intellectual response to the changes brought by the invading armies of Philip and Alexander (*LSE* 162). Consolation could be the answer. Perhaps people naturally seek a permanent unity in the face of change and diversity.

---

[11] The question does not seem to bother Oakeshott here. Later it will. We shall see he finds the unity in the coherence of experience.

Whether this change was precipitated from some particular character of the Greek people, some circumstantial psychological need, or is a permanent characteristic of human beings, what is clear is that Oakeshott saw this change as important to philosophy and was clear about the nature of the change. The search became one of finding the "eternal ground of things", the "unchanging" the *phusis* (in the restricted sense of "the primary, fundamental, persistent substance") or the *arche* ("the 'beginning' or eternal ground of things")(*EGP* 2).

The Physiologists' Search for Systematic Unity

The Ionic School

In Thales, Oakeshott sees the first person to systematically attempt to answer the question, What is the primary thing? Thales "1. Contemplates the physical world. 2. Seeks a principle of unity. 3. Finds it — water. 4. Explains all physical objects in terms of this. 5. And accounts for change and life" (*EGP* 3v). What interests Oakeshott is not the particular conclusion Thales comes to — water — or the explanation of thickening and thinning that attempts to account for change. What interests Oakeshott is the method he pursues. This is what places Thales' reflections at the "dawn of philosophy". It was a time when there was little "trace of a conflict between science and popular belief — religion"; a time when science itself was the attempt to make sense of and unite experience (*EGP* 4). What Oakeshott finds of value in Thales is

> the conception of seeking a principle of unity. It is a 'scientific' (in the widest sense) attitude of mind. It is an enquiry after the ultimately real. There is in it a germ of the true method, though it is not fully mastered or its application freed from the merely arbitrary (*EGP* 3v).

We saw above that the story of philosophy begins in curiosity about all sorts of things and an undifferentiated set of methods for pursuing a search. What seems to unite these searches and makes them worthy of the umbrella title 'philosophy' is that the aim is to make rational sense of and find unity in the diversity of experience.[12]

---

[12] What subsequent thinkers valued in these earlier thinkers, Oakeshott maintained in his Cambridge lectures, was both a method *and* a set of important

Oakeshott's notes on Anaximander show how he thought Thales fell short; how he was far less than free from that which is arbitrary and extraneous to the practice of philosophy. Anaximander's 'daring speculations' lead him to the conclusion that the "primary substance cannot be one of the particular things we see" (*EGP* 3). This move begins to set him into an idealist framework.

> If we explain things by some particular substance or determinate matter, the question arises — whence comes *this* substance? And so the infinite — as the result of a regress of finites. A causa sui; materia prima (*EGP* 3v).

Anaximander therefore locates the first element or cause in what he calls the 'infinite' or 'boundless' (*EGP* 3). Ferrier remarks that what is of merit in Anaximander's system is "its tendency to bring to light the opposition between the finite and the infinite"; the conciliation of the two Ferrier believes is the principle of philosophy (1886, 53).

What seems to strike Oakeshott about Anaximander is the bold nature of his scientific speculations. "The nature of the sun, moon, stars, rain, earth, sea, thunder and lightning etc. He saw that there was no absolute up and down in the world. These were very daring speculations" (*EGP* 3). One might recall Oakeshott's own characterization of philosophy as 'radically subversive' thought: thought that never takes as fixed some set of propositions (*RPML* 141).[13] Anaximander moves in this direction. Our common sense experience points us in the direction that the world is made up of particular materials (air, water, earth, etc.). However, Anaximander is not content with Thales' formulation that the fundamental matter is water. There must be something more basic and more abundant out of which the different particular matters come from. He thus arrives at the boundless or infinite. Both Oakeshott, and Ferrier (1866, 50–51), locate the "germ of the distinction between matter and form" — "genus et differentia" — in the pressing for a primary substance out of which arises particular substances. The notion that what is sought is not an escape

---

conclusions or opinions (CL 4). One of the valuable distinctions Oakeshott took from the ancient Greek language was the distinction between theorizing and a theory: a distinction lost in the phrase "political theory" which Oakeshott claims has resulted confusion and ambiguity. For the last (of many) reference(s) to this vocabulary see *On Human Conduct* (1975, 3n1).

[13] See also Oakeshott (*EM* 2).

from the concrete, particular, experience to some universal, general, reality but a conciliation of the two (a concrete universal), is a persistent tenet of more contemporary idealism.

Anaximenes, though seeming to fall back on a particular substance (air) to explain all things is not understood by Oakeshott to have done so. Rather, in settling on air, Anaximenes seems for Oakeshott to have hit upon a kind of substance having more explanatory power. "In selecting air, A. seems to approach the idea of spirit, or mind πνευμα" (*EGP* 3v). Oakeshott seems to have been impressed by the fragment preserved in the doxological tradition which goes as follows: "Just as our soul, being air, holds us together, so do breath and air encompass the whole world".[14] The unity comes not from a thing as determinate as the water of Thales or as indeterminate as the boundless or infinite of Anaximander, but in something, as Ferrier remarks, "sufficiently indefinite to be universal" and "sufficiently definite to be perceived and understood": a "determinate infinite" (1886, 55). Oakeshott sees in Anaximenes a movement toward the purely logical. "Particular things are the rarification, in different degrees, of the one substance. The conception holds all contraries. It is monistic. A universe. Scientific speculations. The effort to explain the world as it appears to experience". (*EGP* 3). Oakeshott appears to find in Anaximenes a groping towards the understanding of philosophy as the search for unity, not in a particular substance or in a universal substance, but a spiritual, logical or rational unity (hence air as the settled upon substance). And, this unity is an 'explanation' of the world as it appears to 'experience.' This is decidedly Oakeshottian language and signals a grounded experiential approach rather than an other-worldly approach of seeking some reality outside of our experience and an non-materialist approach. It is in the Italic school, and the thinking of Pythagoras of Samos, that this movement takes a more definitive shape and moves from sensual experience to rational experience.

The Italic School

In the thought of Pythagoras we see an "advance, to some extent, from sense to reason, as compared with the Ionics" according to Oakeshott (*EGP* 4v). He notes the communal soci-

---

[14] Cited in Burnet (1908, 77).

ety Pythagoras founded at Kroton and the later influence this may have had on Plato's ideas of communism and the philosopher-king (*EGP* 4v). However, Oakeshott appears more keen to understand Pythagoras the scientist and philosopher. For, as a scientist, Pythagoras "saw that 'release' came from knowledge rather than from ritual" (*EGP* 4). The theoretical advance Pythagoras made was that, while previous "thinkers tried to reduce the world to a physical unity or harmony – P. tried to reduce it to an immaterial principle of number" (*EGP* 4v). The previous Ionic thinkers had focused on their immediate sense experience and material world and attempted to explain that material world in terms of some primary material. With Pythagoras we get a significant turn toward idealism. From the Ionic school we get the idealist concern for some kind of unity, from Pythagoras we get the search for a unity under a non-material entity. Sense gives us particulars (sounds, colors, tastes, etc.). The number one, however, is the same to you as it is to me. It is a part of the truth or reality that is true and real for all human beings. Numbers provide a universal way of attempting to harmonize the different experiences and explanations people have. Quoting Ferrier, "Number is a necessary form of thought under which we place or subsume whatever is presented to the mind" (*EGP* 4v). It is necessary in a way senses are not, for our senses lead us to different conclusions, but numbers are universal – a form of reason or intellect – which leads to truth for all reasoning individuals or intellects.[15] Oakeshott references Ferrier only twice in this portion on Pythagoras and where he does it is instructive.

Oakeshott is impressed with what at first appears a puzzling quotation from Ferrier:

> The whole confusion and misapprehension with which the Pythagorean and Platonic, and many other systems, have at all times been overlaid, have their origin in an oversight as to the kind of truth which philosophy aims at apprehending (*EGP* 4v).

For Ferrier the truth which philosophy aims at apprehending is fairly clear, if a bit abstract. "Philosophy is the pursuit of absolute truth conducted under the direction of reason" (1866,

---

[15] Is this an early intimation of Oakeshott's scientific mode: "the world conceived under the category of quantity"; the world *sub specie quantitatis*? (*EM* 198).

27).[16] But, what is absolute truth and reason for Ferrier? He begins by making the distinction between relative versus absolute truth. Relative truth is true for one mind or truth to our sensible impressions (1866, 8). Absolute truth is true for all minds or truth conceived in relation to intelligence (1866, 9). Philosophy consists of the pursuit of the latter. Rephrasing this understanding, Ferrier says,

> Truth, we may say, is that which is – it is the real; so that, instead of saying that philosophy is the pursuit of the absolute truth, that is, of the truth as it exists for all intelligence, we may say that 'philosophy is the pursuit of the absolutely real, that is, of the real as it exists for all intelligence' (1866, 27).

What is of interest here in terms of the understanding of philosophy is the striking similarity of Ferrier's and Oakeshott's views. Oakeshott distinguishes, in *Experience and Its Modes*, a world of experience which is personal or experience viewed from an individual's perspective (*EM* 68). However, this initial distinction is not as significant as the understanding both Ferrier and Oakeshott share of the character of truth, reality and reason. Oakeshott, like Ferrier in the above quotation, sees truth and reality as inseparable (*EM* 69). By bringing truth and reality closer together, what is being accomplished is to bring truth closer to experience and to make it accessible. If reality is what experience immediately presents to us and truth is something separate, truth gets located someplace further outside, behind, or before our experience. The separation fosters a view that truth resides outside experiential reality; that experiential reality either corresponds or does not correspond to truth. Truth for both Oakeshott and Ferrier is experiential reality fully conceived, and it is approached by subjecting our particular understanding of reality to self-criticism, to critical thinking, or to reason. Reason is taken to be, in its more ancient usage, as a reckoning or a making sense of disparate aspects of our experience. Compare Ferrier's portrayal of how a philosopher approaches another philosopher's work to Oakeshott's understanding of finding that which is true and factual. "What he must be able to say to himself", Ferrier notes of the philosopher, "is this: Such a system, or such a doctrine, or such a prob-

---

[16] This particular formulation of philosophy must have struck Oakeshott for he returns to it later in the notebook. As we shall see, Socrates is said to recover the earlier Pythagorean "desire and value of pure knowledge" that is philosophy.

lem, is not what some individual thinker has chosen to think, or has accidentally thought, but is what thinking itself, in certain circumstances, must inevitably think", and Ferrier speaks of Hegel and Zeller as pioneers in this study of the history of philosophy (1866, 3–4). Similarly, in *Experience and Its Modes*, Oakeshott speaks of the finding of fact and truth as always something to be established or acceded to "truth is the world of experience as a coherent whole, nothing else is true and there is no criterion of truth other than this coherence", or, "fact consequently is achieved only with a coherence of a world of experience", or again, "fact is what we are obliged to think, not because it corresponds with some outside world of existence, but because it is required for the coherence of the world of experience" (*EM* 323, 42).

To return to Pythagoras, what strikes Oakeshott and Ferrier about his system is that he attempts understand the unity of reality, not in terms of a particular substance or a particular intelligence, but in terms of numbers which have a universal quality (not my conception of reality, but the reality for all of us).

The Eleatics

The Eleatics mark a further movement toward seeking unity in thought, rather than either material substances or in mathematical enquiry (*EGP* 5v). Though Xenophanes proceeds in a different fashion: Xenophanes' philosophic contribution of articulating the antithesis of the one and the many, is entangled with his theological reflections for Oakeshott. Oakeshott is so struck by Xenophanes as the author of the conflict between poetry and philosophy that he records a number of fragments which satirically denounce the anthropomorphizing of the gods displayed in Homer and Hesiod (*EGP* 5). Xenophanes is led to a monotheistic conception, being "firmly persuaded of the One and the unity of God" (*EGP* 5v). Philosophically this view involves a dialectical antithesis of the one, which is permanent and perceived by reason and the many and changing sensual world which is "a figment of man's mind" — having "no reality as such and in itself" (*EGP* 5).

Parmenides is given a more thorough treatment than the other Eleatics.[17] Following Burnet, who argues the "great nov-

---

[17] In the notebook Parmenides does not follow Xenophanes in the order in which the actual notes are taken, but does follow the order of development listed on

elty of the poem of Parmenides is the method of argument",
Oakeshott notes that Parmenides begins with common opinion (1908, 205). "But this asserts the existence of what is not"
(*EGP* 6). One might consider how earlier thinkers from Thales
forward tried to unify reality in terms of a substance like water
or air or, in the case of Pythagoras, in terms of number. What
Oakeshott sees Parmenides doing is working out the implications of this view regardless of where they lead. The finding
that all is water or air and that the multiplicity we perceive is
merely the coagulation or thinning out of these primary substances is taken a step further by Parmenides and investigated
for the logical premises involved. He argues that if there is a
primary substance, and this is what is real, then all else must
be illusory and unreal. "What is, is", Parmenides famously
pronounces. If what is is air, then can what is not air be
thought? "No, for if you think you must think something.
Therefore it is nothing" (*EGP* 6). It is Parmenides' radicalism in
pursuing the conclusions of this idea that sets him apart for
Oakeshott. Oakeshott records the fragment that "thought
exists for the sake of what is", which I take to reflect not merely
that thought is necessary for reality but also that thought or
reason can advance toward a truer reality. It is this faith in reason "that enables philosophy to advance" (*EGP* 6). The
method is a radical one of pursuing where thinking leads
regardless of the consequences, and they lead to some extraordinary consequences. Quoting Burnet:

> what is, is a finite, spherical, motionless, corporeal plenum, and
> there is nothing beyond it. The appearances of multiplicity and
> motion, empty space and time, are illusions (*EGP* 6).

Parmenides pushes the Ionic thinking to its logical limits and
in doing so begins to articulate the boundaries of knowledge.

Oakeshott is also interested in the initial moments of
Parmenides' method. He quotes a fragment about where the
investigation begins: "It is all one to me where I begin; for I
shall come back again there" (*EGP* 6). There is a suggestion of
the holistic and universal scope of philosophy that we shall see
is an important element of Oakeshott's concept of education.

---

the first page of the notebook and the order followed by Ferrier in his work. I
have addressed each in the order followed by Oakeshott and Ferrier following
the 'logical development' rather than Burnet's approach which is more historical and more focused on the doctrines that emerge from each thinker.

Oakeshott is impressed with this idea and urges comparison with Spinoza's conception

> Everything that is must be true. Truth may by gained from the close examination of any of our ideas; for all man's ideas are, however inadequate, expressions of reality. It is a monistic conception (*EGP* 6v).

Parmenides, of course, never took his philosophic bent in the direction of Spinoza, but rather occupied himself chiefly with ontological speculation which was limited to the corporeal, the bodily, or the material, thus Oakeshott's attribution to Parmenides as the 'father of materialism'. Quoting Burnet, Oakeshott notes "the time was still to come when men would seek the unity of the world in something which, from its very nature, the senses could never perceive" (*EGP* 6v). This something else is advanced upon by Herakleitos. What is noteworthy, however, is the holistic approach in understanding the unity of our experience; that there is a unity in this experience and that this unity is changeless and all encompassing. If there is something beyond this unity we cannot know it, and so it does not exist. But, by attempting through reason to know any part of that unity one has an entree into the whole, since all is one and connected.

Oakeshott sees Zeno as continuing in this critical appraisal of our experience of Parmenides but he argues the negative of Parmenides: Parmenides argues 'what is, cannot change', Zeno argued 'what changes, cannot be' (*EGP* 7v). What is of a more significant contribution from Oakeshott's perspective is Zeno's approach. Oakeshott notes in two places that Zeno is the father of dialectic (*EGP* 7v, 7). And, the method of dialectic is characterized in the following way: Zeno "argued from premises admitted by his adversaries and produced different results" (*EGP* 7). As Burnet indicates, the logical puzzles of Zeno appear aimed at the later pluralist Pythagoreans and are directed particularly at the assumption that the unit had magnitude (1908, 362–63). It is the problem of the "infinite divisibility of the line" and the assumption that points in a line must have magnitude that call into question again the possibility of change and are the source of the Zeno's infamous puzzles: that Achilles can never overtake a tortoise, that a flying arrow rests, and that half the time may be equal to double the time.

For Oakeshott, Zeno's dialectic, the pressing of current, logical assumptions to their *reductio ad absurdum* is what is central. If this is what is significant about dialectic, it would appear that dialectic is predominantly, and least in Zeno's hands, a destructive force. As we shall see, Oakeshott does not abandon the positive role philosophy and the role philosophy has in uncovering and exposing errors even in here philosophy is shown as destructive or deconstructivist. Ferrier remarks of Zeno's puzzles that they "show how thought is absolutely at variance with itself, and thus, by bringing the opposition fairly to the surface, they prepare the way for its ultimate conciliation under the presidency of a higher principle" (1866, 102) and Oakeshott will follow this suggestion.

Herakleitos

It is Herakleitos who attempts a synthesis of the one and the many. Though recognizing Herakleitos is working with a purely physical picture, and not a logical one, Oakeshott remarks "his new discovery is the unity of opposites. There is no One without the Many, and no Many without the One. The opposite 'tension' of the Many constitutes the unity of the One" (*EGP* 5) a view, as we saw, anticipated from a more materialist perspective by Anaximenes. So Oakeshott is impressed with this notion of the unity of opposites. This already positions Oakeshott's view of Herakleitos as different from the reading of him as centrally the theorist of change and flux and hence a theorist eschewing any view of an underlying unity or continuity.

Oakeshott is also struck by Herakleitos' theory of change, and links this theory to this tension of opposites doctrine. Instead of positing either a single, unified, unchanging substance or diversity and flux as the true ground of reality, he attempts to account and synthesize the two. Previous thinkers had attempted to locate the permanent (being) in a particular substance and then try to account for change. Herakleitos' novelty is that he began with change. "The universal is change, motion" (*EGP* 5v). Contrary to Parmenides and Zeno, Oakeshott indicates (following Ferrier) change is taken by Herakleitos as the principle; as what is primary and not derivative.

Oakeshott passes over Burnet's long and detailed analysis of Herakleitos' cosmological theory without comment or reference to focus on the theory of change. Unlike the Ionic or Eleatic philosophers, Herakleitos does not begin with the premise that what is true and real is fixed (being) and proceed to account for the change which our senses present to us. Though as equally skeptical as the Eleatics about the senses, for Herakleitos, "the universal is change [and] motion". He "begins with the unfixed, the Becoming" (*EGP* 5v). The philosophy of becoming, "is mainly due to H" according to Oakeshott (*EGP* 5v). Herakleitos' philosophy is an attempt at a synthesis of being and not-being. But, how does Oakeshott understand Herakleitos on this point? There is an important issue here for philosophy, which Plato later had to confront, for the issue has implications for the very possibility of philosophy as a practice. If what is is and cannot change, but what our experience reveals to us continuously is change and movement, then our experience and that change must not be real; it must be illusion or appearance. The difficulty is how one might get from this position of appearance to the position of reality. If our senses are unreliable guides to the truth and the nature of reality then what is left? For Parmenides, who was unable to see that some things might exist which are not had through the senses, the Parmenidian way is that of passive initiation. In what remains of his poem, a youth is led by chariot while the maidens persuade Justice, the guardians of the truth, to open the door. There is no opening of the door by the youth himself. Further, the Goddess then instructs the youth who remains passive throughout the instruction. What could bridge the divide between what is and what is not, what is in constant motion and what is a motionless and finite unity, is precisely something like the Herakleitian theory of becoming.

Ferrier tries to capture the theory with the following mathematical metaphor: being and non-being are particular moments of becoming much like a falling rock has a fixed velocity (being) at any given moment but no fixed velocity (becoming) as it is continuously accelerating. Or, using a slightly different metaphor, Ferrier talks about time. "The present time *is*, it is the limit between the past and future; but it has no calculable duration: in being it is not" (1866, 117–18, 131). While I cannot claim to fully understand these metaphors, what they both share is that both velocity and time cannot be seen, yet are real and unchanging in the midst of the sensual perception of change. The time example is interesting for a reason other than its connection to the critique of the Parmenidean position. Oakeshott was first introduced to philosophy by John McTaggart, a rather eccentric British Idealist, who is linked, famously if not notoriously, to the claim that time does not exist. If, thinking along the lines of Parmenides' 'what is is', one might see how McTaggart's position might not be so radical. McTaggart argued,

> Absolute reality, according to Hegel, is eternal, and cannot be fully realized in any state of the world which is still subject to succession in time. Reality must see and be seen under the highest category only (Robbins 1982, 97).

Both, Parmenides and McTaggart fix a reality that would appear to be outside of the reasonable expectations of average individuals, who live in this workable if not logically satisfying experience of everyday life.

Ferrier's example suggests there is a more adequate way to move from change to un-change, and that way is to move, following Plato's lead, from sensible (changing) to intelligible (unchanging/being). Oakeshott seems to view the matter along the same lines, noting that "H. is sometimes thought to have taken Fire as the universal, and so classed himself with the Ionics". But Oakeshott takes this to be "not important" (*EGP* 5v). Oakeshott appears to see the use of fire as symbolic of the principle of change that Herakleitos ultimately hits upon.

Of the hundred and thirty fragments Burnet records (from Diogenes Laertius), Oakeshott fixes on the fragments that reflect the motion and unity of opposites and the character of wisdom. Wisdom is something difficult to attain and must be self-consciously pursued. One might note the different perspective here than that revealed in Parmenides' poem. Oakeshott records the following fragment: "If you do not expect the unexpected, you will not find it; for it is hard to be sought out and difficult" (*EGP* 5). Or again, "It [wisdom] is to know the thought by which all things are steered through all things" (*EGP* 5). It is not a passive engagement, nor is one chosen and whisked away in a chariot to be let into what are usually closed doors as Parmenides suggests.

Oakeshott links the theory of becoming with Herakleitos' remarks on wisdom to extend Ferrier's analysis. Oakeshott urges the comparison with Plato's conception that "friendship is only among the virtuous" and with Spinoza's conception that "all reasonable men agree" (*EGP* 5). While the recognition

that opposites (up/down, wet/dry, good/ill) are "inseparable halves of the same thing" and Herakleitos' theory of
becoming introduces a theory of relativity that "prepares the
way for Parmenides [sic]" and his doctrine that 'man is the
measure of all things' (*EGP* 5) this is not the final reading
Oakeshott gives to Herakleitos. The perception of the unity of
the many and the invoking of Spinoza here implies something
a bit different about the understanding Herakleitos has of the
unity and being of the universe.

Oakeshott does not make a definitive notation about how he
understands Herakleitos on this point, but he identifies wisdom with the "the perception of the unity of the many" (*EGP*
5). There are not just opposites in tension and change, the
change and the tension are part of a unity that supercedes
these. Of the many fragments Oakeshott references by number
on this point, he records two in full: "The waking have one
common world, but the sleeping turn aside each into a world
of his own" and "It is not meet to act and speak like men
asleep" (*EGP* 5v). What is of interest is the ethical component
of the latter fragment (it is inappropriate to turn a way from
the difficult search for unity), and the connection made with
what binds and connects us. How are we to understand this?
What gives us a "'common' world and experience?" One way
to make sense of these fragments is that Herakleitos is saying
that those who are arguing the two different sides fail to see
how both could be true, or how both hold part of reality that
ultimately encompasses and moves beyond either of the two.
And, further that those who have undergone the hard road of
investigating these things understand this and have a common world while still retaining their own individual worlds,
but not their own worlds as exclusive. As Burnet puts it, "the
'strife of opposites' is really an 'attunement' (ἁρμονία). From
this it follows that wisdom is not a knowledge of many things,
but the perception of the underlying unity of the warring
opposites" (1908, 158).

A further implication is about the character of knowledge. It
is not the quantity of knowledge or the special information we
may passively receive from the Goddess, but a kind of insight
had by penetrating below the surface of any tension. Oakeshott
will later talk of knowledge not consisting of the quantity of
experience but as the acquiring of judgment and with becoming
proficient in different languages of explanation.

There is a remaining puzzle too with Herakleitos that Oakeshott fails to address. Is the common world we share a world by virtue of our *agreeing upon it*, or, is it a world because we have turned aside from our sensual perception of the world and *apprehended* a truer nature of the world through reason? There is a lot of ambiguity here both in Herakleitos and in Oakeshott on the relationship between reason and nature. Burnet says that a theory of logos was not altogether available to Herakleitos (1908, 146n3). However, what is clear is that Herakleitos marks an advance for Oakeshott. He accounts for change, making change the principle. In doing so he posits a view of philosophy as the difficult search for unity not in a particular one but in a more universal one that subsumes the multiplicity our senses present to us. In doing this Herakleitos is understood by Oakeshott, not to be the theorist merely of flux and relativity as he is often taken to be. Rather, he urges us beyond our sense experience to find a unity — a unity that is not wholly divorced from sense experience but a unity that is intimated in that very sense experience.

Extension and Suggestion by Others

Oakeshott's treatment of Emepdokles, Leukippos (and the Atomic School), the later Pythagoreans, and Anaxagoras all tell the story of further extension of another's thinking and some suggestions about where philosophy will go from this point forward, but little in terms of major developments.

Oakeshott treats Empedokles, as Burnet does, as a not very thorough thinker representing "a stage in the transition from Monism to Atomism", despite the fact that Burnet devotes over fifty pages to his cosmological and physiological theories (1908, 270). Ferrier equally devotes little to Empedokles only taking serious notice of his theory of perception that 'like must be known by like', which Oakeshott also records (1866, 150–51, 148; *EGP* 6v). Oakeshott notes that the reflections of Empedokles represent "physical rather than philosophical speculation" (*EGP* 6v). What stands out is that Empedokles signals a point where the "monistic principle is abandoned by philosophers", at least until Plato (*EGP* 6).[18] There is no overarching unity, merely fragmented atomism. What is interesting about this point is that here is a moment of stagnation and

---

[18] See also Burnet (1908, 227, 261)

impasse in the story Oakeshott has told about the development of philosophy. It is an impasse not unlike the one
Oakeshott describes in his own time in his Cambridge lectures. Oakeshott, rather boldly, critiques in his first lecture
Harold Laski and Ernest Barker, who in the previous few years
had been appointed chairs of political science at London
School of Economics and Cambridge respectively. Laski
comes under rather severe criticism in advancing, in his inau-
gural speech, the position that various forms of thinking about
politics (economic, historical, and philosophical) are all 'alternative' ways of thinking about politics (*CL* I:2). This 'pluralist'
picture, as Oakeshott calls it, does not get us very far in trying
to understand the relationship of these different forms of
thinking to each other. Laski says they are equal and alternative ways of thinking about politics without saying much
more.

Oakeshott sees a similar position to that of Laski's advanced
by Empedokles. Empedokles leads the way to the Atomic
School by turning aside into a specialized, physical study (natural science), and more specialized divisions within this
study, rather than the more expansive, monistic treatment a
philosophical approach requires. Parmenides had made it
necessary to come up with an explanation of motion (*EGP* 6).
Empedokles does this by dividing the Parmenidean being into
four root elements and attributing change to the separation
due to 'strife' and the combination due to 'love' (*EGP* 6). These
qualitatively different root elements would give way to the
quantitatively different element(s) of the Atomists. Oakeshott
remarks that though the Atomists (Leukippos and
Democritus) were philosophic in character by insisting on "the
least number of principles to explain the greatest number of
phenomenon", they mark a transition in the history of philosophy (*EGP* 8v). As Oakeshott puts it, "this phase of investigation tends to be superceded. Detailed investigation, science
and medicine, take the place of wider speculation" (*EGP* 8).
Oakeshott notes in his Cambridge lectures that a misreading
of Aristotle is partly responsible for the specialization of thinking. Though Aristotle narrowed the meaning of philosophy to
a study of "the first cause of all things", he had many other
interests (*CL* I:5). Given he wrote and lectured so much about
these different interests it was supposed by later generations

that "all these were 'philosophy'" and this view dominated in circles of learning up until the eighteenth century (*CL* I:5).

A rather cursory treatment is made of Anaxagoras.[19] His uneasy relationship to the political Athens is recounted, and his philosophic contribution is not estimated very highly. "Parmenides' conclusions [are] accepted. 'Nous' is the name he gives to the cause of motion. But it is no more of an explanation than the Love and Strife of Empedokles", and, following Aristotle's judgment, he uses mind as a *deus ex machina* (*EGP* 7).[20]

However, having diminished the use Anaxagoras made of 'nous', Oakeshott follows Ferrier by showing the new direction Anaxagoras points for philosophy. "Final cause. Argument from design. Previous to A. most speculation had been about the beginning and cause of things — A. speculates about the ends and purposes of things" (*EGP* 7v). Oakeshott does not provide any quotations from Ferrier's much starker, and I believe less convincing, case. Ferrier argues that the "recognition of ends or final causes in nature is equivalent to the admission of an intelligent principle as the orderer and director of the universe" (1866, 178). The evidence he brings to bear on this point is Aristotle's comment that when Anaxagoras

> affirmed that Mind is present in nature, just as in animals, and is the cause of order and all arrangements therein, he appeared like a sober man among a crowd of drunkards, compared with the futile theorists who proceeded him (*Metaphysics* A.4).

Given Ferrier's otherwise careful reading and scholarship, his argument here is surprisingly unpersuasive. First, Aristotle is talking about his predecessors on their recognition of the efficient cause. Second, Aristotle is not the most reliable inter-

---

[19] Oakeshott spends little time on the later Pythagorean school of Philolaos, which expanded on the earlier notion that number was the universal element in reality. The notion that things are numbers or things partake of numbers, had to deal with the pluralist theory of Empedokles with his four elements or roots and the Sicilian school of medicine with its understanding of health as a balance of elements in the body (Burnet 1908, 344). What results from the confrontation of ideas that interests Oakeshott is the particular conception of the soul that emerges. "The soul is a harmony or attunement – which is incompatible with any theory that the soul may enter the body, or exist apart" (*EGP* 7). "Fundamentally pluralistic system" (*EGP* 7).

[20] See Aristotle, *Metaphysics* A, 4. 985a18, where Aristotle is reviewing the relative clarity with which previous philosophers were able to distinguish material and efficient causes.

preter of his predecessors.[21] Third, as the previous quotation underscores, Aristotle did not think Anaxagoras the most sure footed philosopher.

Oakeshott appears to take a more balanced view on this point (that speculation may have begun in this direction by Anaxagoras but not begun very well). It is the Sophists, Oakeshott insists, that mark the transition to this new 'teleological' way of treating these questions, an approach that will culminate with Aristotle. What is interesting is that Oakeshott deliberately does not invoke the reading Ferrier gives. Why does Oakeshott choose to attribute the rigor of a teleological position to Aristotle and not Anaxagoras? The question cannot satisfactorily be answered by the notebooks. However, one likely suspect is that Oakeshott simply thought Anaxagoras a lesser thinker than Ferrier did. Another possibility, though hardly sustainable, would be that Oakeshott thought Anaxagoras working toward a position where the monistic understanding of unity is one in thought (mind), without the mind having any kind of directed impetus: that is, Hegel's Mind purged of its eschatological drive.

Summing up the doctrines of the pre-Socratics, Ferrier remarks, with characteristically idealist concerns, "You will observe that with all these philosophers it was the thought of *something*, and not pure thought itself, which was the principle" and though Anaxagoras came closest to this insight, it would take others to articulate this fully. Zeller, whom Oakeshott relies on heavily in the section on the Sophists, indicates a similar transition between Anaxagoras and the Sophists.

> The new principle [nous] which he [Anaxagoras] introduced into physics necessitated an altered direction of enquiry; and thus he is immediately connected with the phenomenon which marks the end of the previous philosophy, and the transition to a new form of scientific thought—viz., the rise of Sophistic opinion (1881, 394).

Echoing Burnet, Oakeshott concludes the notes on the pre-Socratics in the following way:

> Philosophy had now run into a blind alley. So long as it clung to its own presuppositions it had nothing more to say. New problems

[21]   See Taylor (1969) for an oft repeated caution about using Aristotle as a reliable primary source on previous thinkers, especially page 32 on Anaxagoras and Empedokles.

must be raised, those of knowledge and conduct, before further progress is possible — and this was due to the Sophists and Socrates. With them a new era opens (*EGP* 8).

Oakeshott's treatment of the Physiologists focuses on their method, on the character of philosophy, and not so much on each of these theorists' conclusions. He is much less concerned with how accurate a picture of the physical world as the logical development of thought. It might be remarked the significance of these early philosophers comes, for Oakeshott, not from the particular doctrines they promulgated but in their method, in their questions, in their attempt to find a monistic unity in thought. Oakeshott's treatment of the pre-Socratics is rather sympathetic and hardly dismisses the pre-Socratics as naïve metaphysicians who lack the true science. He shares the approach Ferrier has of these authors.

> We have to remember, for one thing, that we, as soon as we were born, have entered on an inheritance of thoughts and of words from which these early thinkers were altogether cut off. They had to think out and to devise what we find already thought out and devised to our hand. What we pass by as rubbish, because we are so familiar with it, was, in its first revelation, a divine spark which enlightened the irrational darkness of man's original nature, and bespoke the presence of a reasoning and reflective mind (Ferrier 1866, 92–93).

It is hard to not fully appreciate this remark reading the pre-Socratics. How different a set of beliefs we have inherited about the physical world, and how difficult it makes entering into the mind of these early thinkers!

Chapter III

The Sophistic Challenge and the Socratic Reply

We have seen how the poets ushered in philosophy, illustrating the doubt and questioning that is the seedbed for philosophy. And, with the pre-Socratic psysiologists we saw the early development of philosophy as a quest for the unity in the multiplicity our senses present to us. The Sophists mark a transition in the development of philosophy and a powerful challenge to what Oakeshott saw as the original impetus for philosophy. The Sophists force a confrontation with some major epistemological questions that leads to a particular understanding of the relationship between knowledge and practice. Specifically, the knowledge the pre-Socratics sought the Sophists saw as useless if not completely impossible to find, and what was needed was to turn toward the knowledge that could help people act more successfully; toward, what Machiavelli would call much later the 'effectual truth' (1985, 61). This answer the Sophists give, to put knowledge in the service of action, Oakeshott sees Socrates as rejecting. The Socratic formulation according to Oakeshott has Socrates place thought above action as an end itself. As he elaborates this clash between Socrates and the Sophists, Oakeshott gives a rather unusual reading of Socrates: Socrates is a social and political conservative, but a philosophical radical and skeptic. This characterization of Socrates fits Oakeshott himself rather well and shows Oakeshott, at a very early age, already attracted to a skeptical and philosophical position quite different from other idealists.

The Sophists: Nature, Convention and the Abandonment of Philosophy

For Oakeshott, the Sophists represent a new moment for phi-losophy. This new dawn or era of philosophy is marked by the changing circumstances in Greece and particularly Athens of the time, according to Oakeshott, and this change had a pro-found effect on the practice and conception of philosophy. The Sophists mark a turning point in philosophy: from physi-cal/cosmological concerns to ethical concerns, from purely theoretical concerns to practical theorizing, and from author-ity to radical skepticism.

The Greek world, and particularly Athens, was on the rise after the victories over Persia and Carthaginia and reached, as Zeller puts it, "a height of prosperity and power, of glory and culture, of which history affords no parallel" (*EGP* 8; 1881, 396). No doubt the superior intellectual advantage the Greeks displayed, both tactically at Marathon and Salamis and tech-nologically with their heavy armor, suggested to them the practical source of their strength and they turned their atten-tion to these sources. As Zeller puts it, "just because men had gone so far, they found it necessary to go further" (1881, 396). "New needs [were] felt", Oakeshott indicates. When the Greeks turned their attention to the educational apparatus available they found it wanting. "The old philosophy did not satisfy"; "Education was still confined to music and gymnas-tic" (*EGP* 8).

It is with these changes in mind that Oakeshott begins this section of his notes with a seemingly unremarkable quotation from Zeller.

> Philosophy, until about the middle of the fifth century, was con-fined to the small circles which the love of science had assembled in particular cities around the authors and representatives of physical theories (*EGP* 8).

Zeller here is making two important points in his work that are of interest to Oakeshott about the character of education. Zeller points out that "scientific enquiry concerned itself but little with practical life", which seems to account for the fact that the "principle that practical capability is conditioned by scientific culture was, generally speaking, quite alien to antiq-uity" (1881, 394-95). The educational system, if one can be said to exist, consisted of either an education in music, gymnastics, and some elementary arts, or of these small schools of thinkers who devoted themselves sometimes to practical arts like medicine and mathematics; but also to cosmological and theological speculations, and what we call today theoretical physics. "Everything further", Zeller notes, "was left to the unmethodical practice of life, and to the personal influence of relatives and fellow citizens. Even politics and the art of oratory, so indispensable to a statesman, was learned in the same manner" (1881, 396).

Though this unsystematic education had served the Greeks—and particularly Athens—well, producing figures like Themistocles and Pericles, the desire was felt for a methodological way to train individuals for further success both individually and collectively commensurate with Athens' new status. This want was seemingly supplied by the Sophists. "The education they offered was suited to the times—how to get on in the world" (*EGP* 8v). It was the Sophists' understanding of education and their method of education that marks for Oakeshott at once a further advance for philosophy and a moment when, as Oakeshott rather starkly puts it, "philosophy is infected" (*EGP* 8-9).

The Sophists hold, for Oakeshott, an understanding of philosophy that is deeply compromised if not unhealthy. The infection sets in with the Sophists' radical doubt which, ironically, is the "first essential for the birth of philosophy" and a chief characteristic of Socratic philosophy, though an aspect Socrates puts it to a very different ends (*EGP* 8-9). Oakehsott comments that

> Philosophy had gone through all possible explanations—change and unchange, plurality and unity etc. Each was put forward and provoked its opposite—surely all speculation is vain. And Sophism was born (*EGP* 9).

It is this absolute doubt that leads the Sophists to a particular doctrine about human beings and influences the character of the education they provide.

Oakeshott has a list of notable Sophists: Protagoras of Abdera, Gorgias of Leontium, Prodicus, Hippas of Elis, Thrasymachus of Chalcedon (*EGP* 9). That he spends little time with their beliefs is a bit unexpected. Oakeshott makes notes on their styles and personal character, noting Hippias' vanity and superficial literary efforts and the boastful, avaricious, and selfish character of Thrasymachus. He remarks how they take pay and are educational nomads. When he does say something about their teachings his notes point in a clear direction. Protagoras' appropriation of Heraclidian motion and the dualism of the Eleatics lead him to the conclusion that "man can only understand what he can, there is no objective truth—only subjective opinion" (*EGP* 9v). Gorgias' adoption of the Eleatic position that nothing exists led Oakeshott to label him an 'intuitionist' (*EGP* 9v). Philosophically, the doubt of the Sophists leads to the Protagorean doctrine that "man is the measure of the universe", which "destroys objective and essential qualities" (*EGP* 8v). This has profound implications for the understanding of education and philosophy.

In terms of education, this doctrine marks a transition already intimated that education is to take a decidedly practical turn: Sophistic education will be "a school for politics" (*EGP* 10). Oakeshott notes a

> gradual change in emphasis in the study of science and philosophy. First men studied nature and dabbled in practical politics, but the Athens of the fifth century, studies politics and sees science as a storehouse from which to draw analogies (*EGP* 10v).

These are analogies, Oakeshott says, not truth or guidance: analogies presumably because, as we have seen, there is no objective truth in the Sophistic position. The doctrine that 'man is the measure of all things' having destroyed objective and essential qualities (*EGP* 8v) naturally fits with a Sophistic education that turns away from dialectical investigation of the nature or essence of a thing to eristic disputation. Quoting Zeller, Oakeshott notes,

> Instead of an objective interest in the knowledge of things, there is only the subjective interest in the exercise of a formal art of thought and speech, and this must find its sole task in the confuting of others, when once any positive conviction of its own is renounced (*EGP* 10).

As such, the Sophists showed a "disregard of scientific investigation" in the disinterested sense of the early psyiologists, and became the "first to develop a systematic scepticism" (*EGP* 10). Education becomes a means and a technique, knowledge becomes, in its narrowest sense, power.[1] Oakeshott recognizes

---

[1]   Oakeshott's reflections on the sophists may be an early identification of what he would later distinguish as 'technical' versus 'practical' types of knowledge. The former is a technique capable of being formulated into rules and written

this shift, not only as the source of the "dishonesty and false subtlety which is now associated with the name [Sophist]", but also as a "turning point in the history of philosophy" (*EGP* 10).

Philosophically this doctrine inverts the picture Zeller has given us of the relationship between science (philosophy) and practice held by the early physiological schools. Practical capability becomes conditioned on scientific knowledge. But it also gives us a particular picture of what knowledge one is capable. Oakeshott devotes a good deal of space in the notebook to exploring the philosophical, the psychological, and the ethical importance of the Sophistic doctrine that 'man is the measure of all things'.

The circumstances of Athens, as a growing imperial power, as a commercial center, and as an unusually curious people, no doubt brought Athenians in contact with many different customs and ideas. The Sophists seized upon this diversity and attempted to explore just what is natural and what is conventional to man. "Nature is considered as being the primary master of man, whose laws he must first obey—society, his secondary master. When they conflict, nature must be obeyed" (*EGP* 10v). This, according to Oakeshott, is how the Sophists understood the relationship between nature and convention. However, Oakeshott thinks the sophists conceived nature rather narrowly. Where later thinkers like Hutcheson ascribed too much of a 'moral sense' to human beings, the Sophists ascribed too little and are the progenitors of later sensational thinkers like Locke, Bentham, and those of the French eighteenth century (*EGP* 10v).[2] "Sensation, alone appertains to 'natural' man—pain and pleasure. Passions, desires etc." (*EGP* 10v). Ethically this translates into the notion that "the 'morals' of natural man are based in 'nature'. The morals of society are 'mere convention'" (*EGP* 10v). The political import of this reasoning is clear.

Philosophy "was already the foe of traditional religion" as we might recall from the early treatment the physiologists gave to Hesiod and Homer. "Now", with the Sophists "it

down. The latter is a practical judgment only acquired over a period of time thorough apprenticeship to a proficient practitioner (*RIP* 12–17). The importance of the latter for Oakehsott fits neatly with this reading of Socrates as a social conservative as we shall see.

[2]   One is inclined to include Hobbes in this list. Oakeshott does not. Perhaps this is an early indication Oakeshott would not follow the typical path of interpreting Hobbes.

turned against social custom etc." (*EGP* 8). In doing so, the Sophists reflect a fundamental shift from the natural philosophy of the physiologists to the ethical concerns which were to play a major role in philosophy ever after. Quoting Barker, Oakeshott notes

> Nature was conceived by these thinkers on a teleological scheme — not, however, as fulfilling an immanent end, but of having for its aim and object the setting of an example to man. In this way, the transition would appear to have been finally made from physics to ethics. If matter was still considered, it was only considered in order to arrive at conclusions about man (*EGP* 10v).

Oakeshott credits the Sophists with being the first to clearly raise the question 'What are the grounds of obligation?' He equally credits them with not supplying an adequate answer to this question (*EGP* 10v). In fact, despite the Sophists being the first to "relate all the different subjects of study and treat them as a whole", despite their willingness to question all assumptions and move philosophical questions into a realm of ethics, Oakeshott treats the Sophists, as Socrates does, as clever if not very ingenious protagonists akin to the Encyclopaedists.

> Their part was to doubt, to breakdown, criticize, laugh to scorn. But they had nothing new to offer. As the Encyclopaedists attacked orthodoxy first and ended by decrying all religion, so the Sophists attacked popular religion, gods of the day, but failed to put anything in its place. Sophistry is the culmination of the revolt of philosophy from popular superstition (*EGP* 10).

Oakeshott sees this as a laudable if inadequate revolt. "The Sophists seized upon and enforced the antithesis" and this sets the stage for Socrates, Plato, and Aristotle who attempt to resolve this dialectic (*EGP* 10).

Socrates and the Supersession of Sensation

The history of philosophy up to the point of Socrates has been characterized by the attempt to satisfy one's curiosity about the world (a world in which traditional/mythical explanations were increasingly unsatisfying). This curiosity manifested itself in a study of the natural/physical world seeking some material unity. When applied to human affairs by the Sophists, this critical questioning about what was natural resulted in an understanding of human beings as naturally sensuous creatures united politically and morally merely by a set of conventions. "*Sensation* alone appertains to 'natural' man — pain, pleasure. Passions, desires etc", Oakeshott understands the Sophists to be saying (*EGP* 10v). From this position arises the ethical belief that the source of one's obligations is nature: one must follow 'nature' above that which is conventional.

It is through Socrates' confrontation with the Sophists over the primacy of sensation and the distinction between *physis* and *nomos*, that we can better understand how Oakeshott understood his philosophical project, what he took to be the significance of Socrates' thinking, and to make sense of his early concerns about the nature of the engagement of philosophy itself. Oakeshott, like Socrates, confronts a similar epistemological problem. And, the way they both solve this problem results in markedly similar conclusions about the character of human beings, the nature of the educational engagement, and the relationship human beings have with the state.

For Oakeshott, Socrates is a critical figure in the history of political thought. He developed a line of enquiry as subversive as the Sophists developed yet as detached and specialized as some of the early physiologists. Socrates is faced with a choice: "fall back on the old traditional beliefs", those preached by the civil authorities (and one might add the playwrights like Aristophanes), or "find better arguments" as attempted by the Sophists and before them the physiologists. Socrates "chose the part of the Sophists rather than that of the blindly orthodox", preaching "freedom of enquiry" (*EGP* 11v). There is a point of congruence, as was noticed at the time and since, between Socrates and the Sophists on their joint concern with seeking what is more permanent or 'natural' in human conduct. However, Oakeshott sees Socrates having made a radical break with the Sophists by pursuing the intimations of earlier physiologists and the meaning of customary moral precepts. While the "Sophists said 'Assert yourself,'" "Socrates returned to 'Know yourself'" (*EGP* 11). This shift reflects for Oakeshott a recovery in part of the Pythagorean "desire and value of pure knowledge" (*EGP* 11). Oakeshott quotes a long passage from Barker on this point:

> He [Socrates] drove home the hard and direct lesson that man should live by known rules; and so far as this was the burden of

his teaching he was a Sophist of the Sophists. But he differed from the Sophists in not attempting to teach new canons of conduct. Far from endeavouring to preach a new rule of self-assertion, which would revolutionize old standards, he sought to elicit from the ordinary conduct of men a clear conception of the rules, by which they already acted. He wished to analyse carefully the duties of life, and to arrive at a clear conception of their meaning: he did not wish them to bring a new conception, acquired from some other source, and remodel life by its aid (*EGP* 11).[3]

Barker and Oakeshott agree on the moral conservatism implied in Socrates' approach.

> Socrates was a conservative in that he equated the just and the legal. A real loyalty and love of law. There is no such thing as natural justice. What the law commands, that is just (*EGP* 12; compare Barker 1906, 52).

They agree Socrates was also a radical.

> He taught men to think and to question everything. He refused to cease his teaching in spite of prohibition. All except conscience must be under the control of the State. But even life must be given up readily if it is the will of the State to take it (*EGP* 12, compare Barker 1906, 53).

This tension, Oakeshott notes, "even Plato never resolved" (*EGP* 12). By distinguishing practical and moral reflections from philosophical reflections, social conservatism and radical philosophical activity can be made coherently to live together. It is perhaps an indication of our own inability to separate the two, and, of course, our commitment to individualism, that leads to the attractive but anachronistic reading of Socrates as the heroic exemplar of the man versus the state. Socrates makes no such claim. He sees no incompatibility in obeying the law, however wrong, and insisting on questioning the justice of a law. Rather, he sees his questioning as a gift to the city—a gift not easily replaced were he killed.

Oakeshott differs rather substantially with Barker however on the significance of Socrates' conservatism and radicalism. The passage quoted above clearly places the emphasis on knowledge and on drawing out clear conceptions of the rules of conduct by which people live. Barker and Oakeshott clearly

---

[3]   Though hardly corrupting to the meaning, Oakeshott does not record the quote faithfully: modernizing the spelling at points, transposing or dropping direct articles, and replacing 'would' for 'should' in the third sentence (See Barker 1906, 47).

agree Socrates is arguing "you will be better for knowing the rules which underlie your actions" (*EGP* 12). Barker, however, understands the aim of knowing these rules and the betterment that follows largely in moral terms. Barker takes Socrates to have embraced a substantive moral conservatism, where Oakeshott finds a conservatism emanating from the detachment required of a philosopher.

Barker detects a moral aim in the close connection between the Sophists and Socrates. Barker says that the

> age of the Sophists had conclusively shown both the need in which men stood of a teacher, and the need that such a teacher *should give rules of action*. There had been a systematisation in almost every branch of knowledge.

Even cookery and grammar had been made into arts and been the subjects of treatises (1906, 46).[4] For Barker, Socrates is continuing this rationalistic systematization in morals. This is how Barker understands the Socratic maxim 'virtue is knowledge' — by knowing more clearly the rules of action one can act better. "With this moral aim before him, Socrates lived the life not of a philosopher, but of a prophet, in the old Hebrew sense of the word. He was a teacher; but he was a teacher of righteousness to his people, burning with the zeal of his mission" (1906, 47-48). Oakeshott leaves out of his notebook this part of Barker's argument on the practical, moral meaning of Socrates' teaching and focuses instead on what he takes to be the philosophical meaning.

Oakeshott is then well aware of the possibility of understanding Socrates as predominantly a moralist, and sees the injunction to 'know thyself' to carry this meaning. Barker understands Socrates merely to be urging a more informed reiteration of the injunction inscribed on the Delphic Oracle: *really* understand your place in the social and cosmic order; avoid hubris about your capacities as a human being. Oakeshott, however, following Ferrier, places the emphasis on the philosophical meaning Socrates attributes to this injunction. Instead of asking what are the strength and weaknesses, the limits and extent, of your capacities, the question Socrates asks according to Oakeshott and Ferrier is "What is the *nature*

---

[4]   Emphasis added. One cannot help but recall Oakeshott's use of the example of cookery as a way to distinguish technical and practical knowledge in *Rationalism in Politics and Other Essays* (1991, 12–13).

of your capacities?" (*EGP* 11v; Ferrier 1866, 218). It is not the quantity but the quality, the nature, or the essence that makes this a philosophical injunction. And, when Socrates follows this injunction he finds the Sophistical answer altogether wanting.

The Sophists asked the question what is natural to man and found sensation. "Is sensation the be all of 'natural' man?" Oakeshott has Socrates asking (*EGP* 11v). And in a series of notes (that is remarkable for its similarity to the argument made a decade later in *Experience and Its Modes*), Oakeshott and Socrates reply, emphatically, 'No'. "Socrates", Oakeshott notes, "tries to show that *thought* or *thinking* is as natural to man as sensation". "Socrates came to the conclusion that *thought* and not *sensation* was the distinctive characteristic of man" (*EGP* 11v). The Sophists focused on the sensation itself and not on the source of sensation and the process by which one comes to have the sensations they have. "The Sophists had tended to leave out *thought* or *thinking*. They thought, but did not examine the nature of the process [of thought itself]" (*EGP* 12v).

Sensation alone provides a disparate multiplicity of individual experiences; a chaos of experiences that have no meaning or continuity. One recalls a passage in the *Phaedo* where Socrates speaks of the warring confusion of desires and sensations that causes such internal uproar in the soul that the soul is distracted from exercising its capacity for reason.[5] It is reason that provides the harmony, the clarity, the stability, and the unity to our experiences. The turn toward the *logoi* is a difficult freeing of the soul from the body and thus philosophizing is a kind of dying (66b).

Oakeshott makes a similar judgment about sensation in his notebook. "*Sensations, per se*, are isolated, individual, particular, singular, having no *memory* — save merely reflex reaction" (*EGP* 11v). One of the first and elementary concerns Oakeshott has in his work of a decade later (*Experience and Its Modes*), is this distinction between sensation and thought. He says, perhaps thinking back to Socrates and the Sophists, "A distinction, which goes back to the beginning of reflection upon the character of experience, has been maintained between the

---

[5]   One might also usefully compare the characterization of democracy and the democratic soul in Book 8 of the *Republic* (560d–561e).

senses and the mind, between sensation and thought or judgment" (*EM* 11).[6] Oakeshott is eager to show early on in his first major work that the distinction is misleading and false. In making the distinction, the given in sensation is usually taken to be

> isolated, simple, exclusive, and wholly unrelated; transient, inexpressible, unsharable and impossible of repetition. In sensation (thus conceived) there can be nothing more than a bare 'this is', in which the 'this' is utterly indeterminate, without name or character, and the 'is' is limited to merely 'here' and 'now' (*EM* 13).

Oakeshott sees Socrates as confronting a similar epistemological problem vis-à-vis the Sophists and coming to a remarkably similar conclusion.

Oakeshott and Socrates (as Oakeshott reads him) are making a similar point about taking sensation as the primary starting point of our experience; taking sensation as the raw data which is in turn reflected upon, categorized, organized, and upon which judgments are passed, etc. Even something as simple and as apparently unmediated an experience as pain is never isolated and exclusive. "Mere sensation we can *take to be* involuntary—but it is an abstraction" (*EGP* 11v, emphasis added). "To *think* pain as well as *feel* it—that is something different", Oakeshott notes. Thought, of which sensation is a variety for Oakeshott and Socrates, does not have this abstract quality. "*Thought, per se*, is never isolated, merely individual; it depends upon 'experience'. It knows nothing *per se*. It depends on mental relations—a 'whole' of experience" (*EGP* 11v). Compare a similar passage in *Experience and Its Modes*:

> To be conscious of something is, in some degree, to recognize it; and recognition involves us at once in judgment, in inference, in reflection, in thought. Consciousness, moreover, requires a subject which stands above mere momentary states of sensation; it requires, at least, a body of related experiences in some degree organized and harmonious. Nothing, in short, can maintain the claim to be in experience which presents itself in utter isolation, alone, without world, generation or relevance. Experience is always and everywhere significant (*EM* 14).

---

[6]   Oakeshott also had before him the realism of G.E. Moore, who all but displaced idealism at Cambridge. Moore was teaching at the time Oakeshott was a student and lecturer at Cambridge, and held that sense data was independent from an object itself. The view leads, when combined with a belief in universals, to the view that truth and reality lie behind sensuous experience, thus a correspondence theory of truth (Reese 1980, 369).

Experience, Oakeshott is saying in his notebook and more systematically in *Experience and Its Modes*, is not just infected with thought or mediated through thought, or something that thought is brought to bear upon, but is thought itself in different varieties. This requires a self wholly made up of thought: a being that is a complex of interrelated and significant experiences; what Oakeshott will later call in *On Human Conduct* a 'reflective intelligence' (1975, 36–37). It is thought itself and a thinking, reflective being that is the source of the unity in the world.

> The view I propose to maintain is that experience is a single whole, within which modifications may be distinguished, but which admits of no final or absolute division; and that experience everywhere, not merely is inseparable from thought, but is itself a form of thought. It is not, of course, wrong to attempt an analysis of experience, to distinguish (for example) sensation, reflection, volition, feeling and intuition; the error lies in supposing that in so doing we are considering activities which are different in principle and can be separated from one another finally and absolutely. They are the products of our analysis, lifeless abstractions which (like all such) call out to be joined to the concrete whole to which they belong and whence they derive their nature. All abstract and incomplete experience is a modification of what is complete, individual and concrete, and to this it must be referred if we are to ascertain its character. And thought or judgment, as I see it, is not one form of experience, but is itself the concrete whole of experience (*EM* 10–11).

Oakeshott sees Socrates coming to a similar conclusion. Socrates saw clearly that experience and reality were fundamentally a matter of thought and judgment, which led him to the "conclusion that *thought* and not *sensation* was the distinctive characteristic of man" (*EGP* 11v). One is reminded of a passage in *On Human Conduct* almost over forty years later where Oakeshott argues that a necessary postulate of human conduct is reflective consciousness or thought. "Intelligibles emerge out of misty intimations of intelligibility when noticings become thoughts and when, in virtue of distinguishing and remembering likenesses and unlikenesses in what is going on, we come to inhabit a world of recognizables" (*OHC* 3). One of the central characteristics of human beings (or human nature) is that they are the thinking animal; that they are reflective intelligences. This is the source of their freedom for both Oakeshott and Socrates. Socrates insisted on the freedom to think and question, despite being prohibited, and yet also insisted on obeying the law.[7] Oakeshott, in *Experience and Its Modes*, locates human freedom in the same realm. A human being "is 'free' not because his situation is alterable by an act of unconstrained 'will' but because it is an understood situation and because doing is an intelligent engagement" (*EM* 37).[8] There are important consequences that follow directly from the primary and unifying role of thought, for the rest of the Socratic and Oakeshottian philosophies.

The Thinking and Learning Being

Experience is thought. It is not sensation plus whatever thought and judgment bring to the accumulated 'data' of sensation. In *Experience and Its Modes*, Oakeshott makes direct reference to this being Socrates' understanding.

> Thinking, according to the analogy of the *Theaetetus*, is a process of catching not wild birds, not what is outside experience (such as the objects in mere sensation), but tame birds already within the cage of the mind. It is a process of recognition in which we reconsider judgments already in some degree affirmed (*EM* 19)

This idea has major impacts on Socrates' and Oakeshott's further thinking on knowledge and learning, on the nature (*physis*)/convention (*nomos*) controversy the Sophists have raised, and on the understanding of one's relationship to the State.

Socratic Knowledge and Learning

The image of tame birds in a cage Socrates uses in the *Theaetetus* provides insight into his understanding of the educational engagement and the nature of knowledge. Though

---

[7]   The tension between the Socrates of the *Apology* and the Socrates of the *Crito* has been frequently commented upon pointing out Socrates' insistence on questioning the law on the one hand and his defense of the laws he makes to Crito on the other. It is not my project to resolve this tension or to present a full-blown Socratic philosophy of law. However, any resolution of this apparent tension must, as with most of the Platonic dialogues, make special note of the character to whom the argument is made (Crito in this case), and that Socrates' prime interest is the philosophic life. Socrates' thoughts on the obligation to follow law must be seen as of secondary interest to philosophy. In this ranking, Socrates may be on the way to a more procedural understanding of law.

[8]   Oakeshott has a similar recognition of this idea in *On Human Conduct* calling the rational, thoughtful element in human conduct, 'intelligence in doing' rather than either reason or will (1975, 37).

this will get a more extended analysis later on, it is worthwhile making some preliminary remarks about the similar views of Oakeshott and Socrates on education. For both, their understandings of education have an intimate relationship to their theories of knowledge.

Oakeshott is largely taken by the image of tame birds in a cage, for it mitigates against the belief that knowledge and the process by which we acquire knowledge is a piecing together of the various independent experiences we may have. Education is not analogous to a painter's colors or a builder's bricks, Oakeshott says in *Experience and Its Modes* (1933, 19). It is not about the quantity of sense experience, or even with having acquired a specific set of opinions as the knowledge of the pre-Socratics was partly taken to consist.[9] Theaetetus equates perception (experience) with knowledge, which is likely to lead both to the belief that knowledge is purely subjective (that man is the measure), but also to a quantitative assessment of knowledge: the more experience, the more knowledge. This is not the understanding of education Socrates has.[10] Nor do Socrates and Oakeshott hold the view that education is about taking basic sensations as the foundation stones for the rest of experience. A familiar simile Socrates uses, with particular emphases in the *Theaetetus*, is to liken education to giving birth to ideas and the educator as a midwife (149a–151e). The image of tame birds captures this quite well for it is not the number of birds, nor is it the initial catch and catching site of the birds that is significant but the coming to know the birds more fully. Here Oakeshott believes the image is misleading to the extent it presupposes birds once wild. However, the central thrust of the image remains the same.

Oakeshott ends the section on Socrates in his notebook with a series of notes on the central Socratic doctrines, the first of which concerns this epistemological point. "All rational knowledge must be elicited from within the mind. So the Socratic method of education. So, all knowledge is reminiscence" (*EGP* 12). Though this is a familiar understanding of Socratic knowledge, Oakeshott does not take this to mean that the Forms or Ideas are somehow implanted in our souls from the beginning. Even the "doctrine of *Ideas*" is the product of

[9]   See above, Chapter 2.
[10] One might also note how this differs from Aristotle's understanding of education with its emphasis on forming good habits.

thought; of the free, active, and logical attempt to understand what we in some sense already know (*EGP* 11v). This is not a theory of innate ideas Oakeshott indicates. It was only "in later times this appeared as the doctrine of innate ideas" (*EGP* 12).

Oakeshott strikes a similar chord in an essay in the late 1940s on the paradoxical nature of all learning and all reflection. "The root from which all reflection springs is the paradox that we know and that at the same time we do not know" (*RPML* 138). Learning is the process of coming to know better what we in some sense already know. As he says, similarly, much later in *On Human Conduct* "The engagement to understand, then, begins in an already understood: a verdict, or what we ordinarily call a 'fact'. But this verdict is the contingent starting-place of a critical inquiry; it is an understanding waiting to be understood" (1975, 2).

The process of reflection and education for Socrates and Oakeshott is fundamentally dialectical. Oakeshott is explicit about this: "the process of reflection is *dialectical*, a process of considering something recognized as knowledge and supposed to be true, yet considering it with the assumption that it is not true". And, he continues,

> This I believe to be, not merely the character of one particular kind of reflection, but the universal character of all reflection. Unless we reflect there is no world; and when we reflect we engage in this dialectical activity (*RPML* 139).

Compare the notes on Socrates. "*That* man should think he is obliged. *What* he thinks depends on his 'experience'. For thought is not bound down to the *particular* sensation" (*EGP* 11v). In a separate notebook on Plato's *Republic*, Oakeshott remarks that "In Socrates the dialectical tendency emerges and becomes supreme" and then he continues with the following quotation from Zeller:

> In previous philosophy thought had been directed immediately to the object, as such. In the Socratic and post-Socratic systems it was directed immediately to the conception, and to the object only mediately, through the conception . . . . The conception of a thing is only obtained, by observing its various aspects and qualities, by uniting them, by harmonising apparent contradictions, by distinguishing what is lasting from what is changing, in a word, by that constructive criticism, which was introduced by Socrates,

and which was enlarged by Plato and Aristotle (Zeller 1868, 36-37; *Rep I*: 2–3).[11]

The dialectical process is predominantly a logical one where common understandings (conceptions) are interrogated not just as Zeno had done pointing out paradoxes but to come to a better and more complete understanding of concepts that one in some sense already understands. This view of how knowledge is acquired and of what it consists has a powerful bearing on the dispute over what is natural and what is conventional that Socrates imagines the Sophists to be engaged in.

Nature and Convention

We have already seen that Oakeshott believes Socrates to be saying what is natural is not sensation but thought itself. This is the distinctive characteristic of man—human beings are thinking, reflective, or learning creatures. This has some implications for the reformulation of the nature/convention distinction. Oakeshott had said earlier that Socrates follows the Sophists in the attempt to find better arguments by doubting and questioning the traditional beliefs. Socrates is like the Sophists in searching for that which is natural versus that which comes down to us by authority: "the 'natural' should rule" (*EGP* 11v). However, the radical skepticism of the Sophists led to the belief that what was natural was that which is perceived, sensed, felt, and desired by each individual and, therefore, one must follow this nature before the dictates of society which are conventional and not natural.

Socrates has argued, however, that what is natural to man is thought. Socrates recognizes that the "*feeling* of self is exclusive" in the Sophistic sense. This is not, however, the full story. In an intriguing note, Oakeshott urges the comparison of the "controversy between Socrates and the Sophists with that between Hobbes and Cudworth, Butler, etc." (*EGP* 11v). Knowing Oakeshott's later interest in Hobbes, this is a very interesting comparison. Though Oakeshott was to later criticize Hobbes for an inadequate theory of volition, Cudworth and later British Idealists like Ferrier, whom Oakeshott is rely-

[11] The Plato notebooks consist of two, handwritten, notebooks consisting of approximately 150 and 70 pages respectively, dated July 1923, on the Plato's *Republic*. I shall refer to the notebooks as Rep., followed by the first or second notebook (I or II) and then the page number.

ing upon here, had slightly different but related objections to Hobbes.[12] Echoing Rousseau, Ferrier understands Hobbes as failing to recognize the natural sympathy human beings have for one another and rather emphasizing human beings' passions and instincts, which, though an accurate picture before human beings "prior to the dawn of self-consciousness", fails to recognize the natural affection human beings have for one another once self-aware (1866, 251–52). Cudworth objected to what was perceived to be Hobbes's sensationalism and materialism. As one commentator puts it:

> As Plato had developed his theory of knowledge in opposition to the sensationalism of Protagoras, so Cudworth found himself faced with a modern revival of Protagoreanism in Hobbes's contention that knowledge and understanding are 'in us nothing else but a tumult in the mind raised by external things that press on the organical parts of man's body', and that this pressure being what we call 'sensation' 'is *nothing more* than a motion among the particles of the sensing body (Muirhead 1992, 40).

The anxieties that Cudworth had over Hobbes's philosophy are shared, to a limited degree by Socrates and by Oakeshott (and most other British Idealists). The point of connection is on the insistence that the mind is an active participant in the process of knowledge. We have seen this to be one of the concerns of Socrates. Cudworth shares this concern with Socrates over the Sophists and with Oakeshott over Hobbes and other more contemporary 'scientific' (behaviorist, empiricist, positivist) theories of human conduct.[13]

However, Cudworth's further anxiety, which is not shared by Oakeshott, is that the mechanism and sensationalism of Hobbes, not only does not address the ancient metaphysical problem of how order comes from disorder, but fails to recognize 'The' ordering principle in the cosmos. That is, Hobbes's theory fails to recognize the immanent divine will at work in the world, without which "all creatures would be merely *ludibria* and vanity" (Muirhead 1992, 56). There is a moral and religious component to Cudworth's reaction against Hobbes's

---

[12] The criticism of Hobbes lacking a coherent theory of volition is found in an essay, "Dr. Leo Strauss on Hobbes", p. 378, originally published in 1937 in *Politica* 2:364–79 and most recently republished in *Hobbes on Civil Association* (1975) by Liberty Fund.

[13] This remained a concern for Oakeshott, for as late as *On Human Conduct* he is careful to distinguish human 'conduct' that is a reflection of intelligence from behavior which is a reflection of psychological or biological 'causes' (1975, 15).

sensationalism, naturalism and materialism and the Cartesian theism of the time. This is a persistent theme in idealism. We saw earlier that Ferrier attributes to Anaxagoras the early suggestion of a providential universe as a sign of philosophy's progress.[14] Hegel was not initially well received in England in no small part due to the perception that Hegel's thought was anti-Christian. This was one source of Coleridge's and Jowett's, among others, complaints with Hegel. Jowett probably studied Hegel (in German) closer than many others at the time. He at first embraced Hegel and then rejected him. The rejection came in no small measure because of the "absence of a transcendent God or 'beyond' in his philosophy" (Robbins 1982, 31–32).

Oakeshott does not go in this theological direction with his analysis. Ferrier has a concern with this spiritual dimension as well. The concern, however, is directed, as it is with Oakeshott, to the shared nature of reality. If, as the Sophists (and Socrates) say, the natural should rule, and, as Socrates has said, what is natural is thought and thought depends on experience, what is the nature of this experience? The Sophists say (and it is believed by these Idealists, Hobbes says) it is sensation. But experience is a form of thought. And, Oakeshott remarks in his notebook, "experience is essentially 'social'" (*EGP* 11v). This, initially, is a startling line of argument. What could Oakeshott possibly mean in saying experience is essentially social? Surely he does not mean that my thoughts are not mine, that the pain I may feel at the parting of a loved one is not a deeply individual thing. And he does not. The meaning of experience as social follows from what he has said before about thought. Our ideas are certainly ours. Oakeshott would be the last to deny this. However, the question all along has been, 'From whence do these ideas come?' Our thoughts and ideas are not innate things that through introspection we come to behold with more and more clarity — ironically this would make experience a personal and deeply subjective thing. The ideas we have are the ideas we have *learned*. "Experience is a world of ideas" Oakeshott says in *Experience and Its Modes* (1933, 27). It is my world in the sense that it is what I understand the world to be. But, what I understand the world to be is a product of

---

[14]   (Chapter 2 above). For a treatment of the religious and moral concerns of British idealism more generally, see Nicholson (1990) and Boucher (1997). See also Robbins (1982) more specifically on the British Hegelians.

what I have learned to understand the world to be. "He can have come by it only in learning, and in learning he acquires only what he accepts and makes his own in an understanding" (*OHC* 37). What I learn is other ideas, sentiments, practices, feelings, etc., which I have not created but which are deeply infused with meaning. In a 1972 essay on education Oakeshott remarks that education

> is the transaction between the generations in which newcomers to the scene are initiated into the world which they are to inhabit. This world is a world of understandings, imaginings, meanings, moral and religious beliefs, relationships, practices—states of mind in which the human condition is to be discerned as recognition of and responses to the ordeal of consciousness. These states of mind can be entered into only by being themselves understood, and they can be understood only by learning to do so. To be initiated into this world is learning to become human; and to move within it freely is to be human, which is an 'historic', not a 'natural' condition (*VLL* 93).

Experience is essentially 'social' because *my* thoughts are what I have made of the world, which is a complex and interrelated set of other thoughts. Thought itself is what ties people together. It is reason and speech that makes my experience accessible and communicable to another, and capable of being criticized, interrogated, altered, reinterpreted, and made more or less coherent. So, Oakeshott continues in the notebook, "the truly 'natural' is the truly 'conventional'. Man is '*by nature*' social" (*EGP* 11v). The two (*physis* and *nomos*) are not incompatible for Oakeshott or Socrates. The distinction between nature and convention is a crude one for Oakeshott, for it fails to take into account that "man's nature issues in all that he does—and conventions are his handiwork" (*Rep* I:25v).

The Political Animal

That a human being is a thinking, and therefore a social, animal has rather clear political implications.[15] Oakeshott notes,

---

[15] Just how social and just how individual Oakeshott imagines human beings to be has been a source of considerable debate in the Oakeshott literature. The debate has centered around the argument over how Hobbesian (liberal, individualism) versus how Hegelian (culturally and historically imbedded) Oakeshott is. See Franco (1990) especially chapter 5, for the more Hobbesian reading of Oakeshott, and Gerencser (2000) for a very skeptical Hobbesian account. For an excellent account of the continued cultural and moral

for Socrates "the State is the individual writ large" (*EGP* 12v). What is interesting is how profoundly Oakeshott understands Socrates to tie these epistemological insights to the political and moral realm. And, though he makes Socrates out to be less of a moralist than Ferrier does, he clearly sees the political and moral implications of these ideas. One might note, however, these moral implications are secondary to the task of philosophy as Oakeshott reads Socrates. Socrates (and Plato as we shall see) are of interest to Oakeshott because they, like the pre-Socratics, were focused on the logical or necessary truths; the concepts themselves, and less on practical results. Oakeshott clearly sees the implication of the one for the other. Ideas have consequences, but the consequences are incidental and not the focus of the philosophic activity.

In this context, one cannot help recalling the close connection that is drawn in the *Republic* between the nature of the regime and the nature of the individual souls that comprise the regime, beginning with the method Socrates proposes to find justice by seeing it in the larger (city) and relating it to the smaller (soul) (368d). There is also the claim in the *Statesman* that the true statesman is a physician of souls (309c–e), and in the *Gorgias* true politics is the making of good souls (521a). Or, again, in the *Apology*, one recalls Socrates presenting himself as the new hero, the new Achilleus; a gift to Athens worthy of free meals in the Prytaneum (28c, 31b, 36d). How is Oakeshott going to confront this mixture of moral and philosophical concerns in Plato? This is the subject of Chapter IV. We shall see that Plato is treated very differently than Socrates, the latter of whom is treated, as we have seen, as preeminently a philosopher and more detached from practical concerns, while the former is treated as a reformer and a philosopher with neither clearly prevalent. Oakeshott ends his notes on Socrates on just this note.

In a list of Socratic doctrines at the end of Oakeshott's notes on Socrates, Oakeshott again resists reading Socrates as primarily a moralist. He does argue that "virtue is knowledge, vice is ignorance" (*EGP* 12). However, "A man's chief ignorance is ignorance of his nature" (*EGP* 12). Ferrier connects this ethical theory much more closely to an ethical teaching than

situatedness see Coats (2000, chapter 3). This issue will be more directly addressed in the chapter on Plato.

Oakeshott does. The ethical theory may change behavior: knowing what is involved when making any moral choice, may allow one to choose better. But is the equation of virtue and knowledge meant to be "a restraint laid upon the natural lusts and passions of the soul" as Ferrier claims (1866, 271)? Oakeshott notes that the

> objection sometimes brought against this [doctrine equating virtue and knowledge], that if it were believed it would sap all moral courage and endeavour of its strength is no objection; for this is an ethical theory, and does not stand or fall on its effect in practice (*EGP* 12v).

Chapter IV

Platonic Knowledge and Platonic Conduct

The substantial body of Oakeshott's published work can be characterized as devoted to questions about the character of knowledge and experience and how knowledge is acquired.[1] Indeed, it would be no exaggeration to say that one of Oakeshott's persistent and central concerns in all of his writings was to understand what he was in fact doing, namely learning and teaching the history of political philosophy. Plato plays a dominant role in Oakeshott's continuing investigation of philosophical knowledge about politics, and Plato's thought is represented as a mistaken way of understanding the character of knowledge, a mistake made both in Plato's time and in our own.[2] Interestingly, it is a mistake Oakeshott must have thought his idealist predecessors made for the path he charts is very different from theirs. Oakeshott's published writings on Plato and his notebooks on Plato show the different path Oakeshott took, a path that much more radically sepa-

---

[1] Oakeshott's first book *Experience and Its Modes*, as he says in the introduction, is "to discover the main implications of this conception of philosophy", of philosophical experience as experience "without presupposition, reservation, arrest or modification" (1933, 2–3). The bulk of this work is devoted to understanding different 'modes' of experience, and more crucially the limited explanatory power of each mode. The title essay in *Rationalism in Politics* (1991), among numerous others, and the essays in *The Voice of Liberal Learning* (1989), are concerned with different kinds of knowledge, the character of knowledge, how knowledge may be acquired, and the impact on human conduct. And, the first essay in *On Human Conduct* is how to 'theorize', how to gain knowledge specifically on human conduct.

[2] Oakeshott remarks in his LSE Lectures on Plato that Plato's understanding of knowledge, as articulated in his doctrine of ideas, and the conclusions he draws from the doctrine "have never been far below the surface of Western European thought" (*LSE* 141).

rates theory and practice than either Plato or his contemporary idealists did.

The notebooks, however, are a much more subtle and generous reading of Plato than Oakeshott's published work. The notebooks show what can only be described as a critical ambivalence Oakeshott had toward Plato. Oakeshott was drawn to what he understood to be the more Socratic and philosophical side of the *Republic*. But, he saw Plato's reforming zeal both distracting him from the philosophical pursuit and leading him to false conclusions. Oakeshott's treatment of the character Cephalus in the *Republic*, and his rather unorthodox reading of the Platonic Forms reveals that Oakeshott was in substantial agreement with the Socratic method that Plato adopts but that the conclusions Plato comes to are overly optimistic about the power and the scope of philosophy. Particularly Oakeshott's treatment of the Forms or the doctrine of ideas shows Plato to advance philosophy by further refining its method and aims, yet, at the same time, depicts Plato as setting philosophy back in two important ways. First, the importance Plato puts on the method as well as the conclusions marks a return to the pre-Socratic view of philosophy as both a method *and* a *set of opinions*. Secondly, the deliberately practical character of Sophistic thinking, which Socrates was shown in the previous chapter to move away from, is embraced by Plato.

Published Treatment of Plato

In the most sustained treatment of Plato in Oakeshott's published work in *On Human Conduct* Oakeshott is critical not of the image of the educational endeavor but of the character of the knowledge, the type of knowledge, Plato believes to be the result of the agonizing ascent out of the cave.

> According to Plato (in some accounts, at least), the theorist who now reluctantly returns to the cave from this greatest of all intellectual adventures carries with him an unconditional understanding of the world in terms of its ultimate postulates (or, as he says, its 'causes'). This understanding, it goes without saying, is vastly superior to that of the cave-dwellers. But it is represented as something more than merely superior. It is alleged to be a complete *substitute* for that and for every other conditional understanding. Thus, the theorist returns, not with something useful in his pocket (as a man might carry a copy of Horace to console him

as he goes to prison, to exile, or to war), but with a gift of inestimable value to mankind: a definitive understanding and language to supersede and *to take the place of* all other understandings and languages (*OHC* 29).

Or, consider Oakeshott's essay "Political Discourse" (*RIP* 70–95), where he argues political discourse (and practical discourse more generally), is unavoidably about causes, consequences, beliefs, probabilities, and contingencies, none of which could be fully known in advance of making a choice. He distinguishes and sharply contrasts practical political thinking (deliberative discourse) from 'demonstrative discourse', the latter of which he sees Plato as the progenitor.

> Plato is the father of demonstrative discourse . . . He understood political activity to be the pursuit of human excellence or *dikaiosune*, and the idea of 'justice' provides a universal and unchanging standard by which the merit of all actions may be determined. He recognized knowledge of the idea 'justice' as genuine knowledge released from the uncertainties and relativities of *doxa*; and as the necessary and sufficient condition of political discourse, which thus could become demonstrative argument governed by 'ideology' composed of a single idea given the status of an axiom (*RIP* 23).

In short, Plato, on this reading, is the father of Rationalism: the father of the belief that to act rationally is to engage in "behaviour in which an independently premeditated end is pursued and which is determined solely by that end" (*RIP* 102). In Plato's language it is the belief that once one beholds the 'Good' — the whole system and set of relations between the Ideas — the 'Good' is capable of directing our actions and can be the criteria for determining good and bad, rational and irrational actions.

Or again, consider Oakeshott's reading of Platonic contemplation (*theoria*), in his celebrated essay "The Voice of Poetry in the Conversation of Mankind" originally published in 1959. There he argues that the description of contemplative activity as "the activity of copying ideal models (and therefore entailing a 'vision' of the models to be copied) . . . reflects some observed condition of human experience", but it misidentifies that experience: aesthetic experience is taken for philosophical experience (*RIP* 521 and 516n13).

> By understanding 'poetry' as a craft, and craft as an activity of imitating ideal models, he [Plato] followed a false scent which led him to the unnecessary hypothesis of non-image-making, 'word-

less' experience, namely, that of 'beholding' the ideal models to be copied (*RIP* 516n13).

All of these references reflect what Oakeshott thought Plato was arguing about the relationship between philosophical knowledge and action. Plato's view is that in order to engage in any activity, whether horse-training, building a chair, or political activity, one *must* have an understanding of the end or the idea the activity aims at prior to engaging in the activity. In the case of politics (which may in fact be very different from building a chair), a rational and just regime cannot even get off the ground unless the just regime (justice itself) is clearly envisioned in advance. Only philosophers seek what is just and see the whole and therefore are the ones uniquely qualified to rule.[3]

Oakeshott's own thinking, in his published work, is in direct contrast with this 'Platonic' conception of what constitutes genuine knowledge. He is critical, in this same essay on poetry, of Plato's view of *theoria* as image-copying and not image-making (*RIP* 516n13). He is critical, to put it slightly differently, of Plato's failure to recognize the creative element in human activity, a criticism made in M. Foster's book *The Political Philosophies of Plato and Hegel* (1935). Oakeshott reviewed this book saying it was "the most profound and illuminating contribution to the literature of political philosophy which has appeared in recent years" (Oakeshott 1935b, 74). Oakeshott makes a similar point much later in his LSE Lectures. "There is, then, no place in Plato's world for an activity of 'free creation': all is copying, and you cannot copy without a known model", that is an Idea (*LSE* 140). There are obviously huge implications for viewing human beings as either fundamentally imitative beings or as creative beings, but before one even addresses that issue, what is implied in being an imitative being is that there is something to be imitated. For Plato these are the forms and, as we have seen, it is the forms that give rise to correct action for Plato, but not for Oakeshott.

Oakeshott's critique of Plato, in these published works, is a reflection of a more general critique that ideals are the spring of activity and action, and that ideals constitute the only form

---

[3]   This is the story Oakeshott tells of Plato in his LSE Lectures on Plato. In the two lectures directly on Plato, Oakeshott divides his treatment of Plato into one lecture on Plato's "intellectual apparatus" or his doctrine of ideas, and the other to the argument and conclusions of the *Republic* (*LSE* 145–46).

of genuine knowledge and learning. As he says in a short essay on the idea of the university published originally in 1951, "It is a favorite theory of mine that what people call 'ideals' and 'purposes' are never themselves the source of human activity; they are shorthand expressions for the real spring of conduct, which is a disposition to do certain things and a knowledge of how to do them. Human beings do not start from rest and spring into activity when attracted by a purpose to be achieved". Echoing Aristotle, Oakeshott continues, "To be alive is to be perpetually active. The purposes we attribute to particular kinds of activity are only abridgements of our knowledge of how to engage in this or that activity" (*VLL* 95). There is no question that this is a very different perspective than the Platonic one, at least the Plato of Oakeshott's published writings. For Oakeshott, practice comes before theory, and what gives rise to any given practice is a 'disposition' to engage in that practice and the knowledge of how to do it. Theory is an attempt to understand and describe the practice itself and lacks the power to give rise to the practice. A stark contrast between Plato and Oakeshott emerges, then, in Oakeshott's published writings. There is also a contrast to be noticed between Plato and Socrates. Plato's epistemological position is at odds with the reading that emerged of Socrates in Chapter 3 as a social and moral conservative. Socrates was understood as seeking to understand, to know thyself, rather than to be engaged in the struggle for power that necessarily constitutes the political way of life. This contrast between Plato and Socrates is on dramatic display in the notebooks on Plato.

Notebook Treatment of Plato

The understanding of Plato in the notebooks is much more nuanced than the Plato of Oakeshott's published writings. Plato's thought in the notebooks is depicted as embodying alternative and conflicting understandings of the quality of and transmission of knowledge. One of the conflicts arises from Plato too hastily dismissing the knowledge in the cave. Oakeshott's reading of the character of Cephalus draws this out, and shows how Plato left unresolved his view that habit, training, experience, and external conditions are crucial, and his belief in the transformative power of beholding the 'Good'.

For Oakeshott, the character of Cephalus represents the "'gathered experience of a good man of the generation which is passing away', so Socrates comes to learn from him" (Nettleship 1897, 15; *Rep I*:10).[4] Aristotle, whom Oakeshott references here, suggested in his *Nicomachean Ethics* this is what philosophers and other should do: "We must attend, then, to the undemonstrated remarks and beliefs of experienced and older people or of intelligent people, no less than to demonstrations. For these people see correctly because experience has given them their eye" (1143b11–14).

Oakeshott sees no irony in Socrates coming to learn from Cephalus. He no doubt is aware that as a metic arms merchant Cephalus is attempting to give what is due to the Gods and others, supposing those myths he learned in youth might be true and attempting to make amends now as he sits on the threshold of old age. However, Oakeshott, following Nettleship, understands Cephalus to be "intuitively in his life and action, what Plato desires all men to become through philosophy" (*Rep I*:10; 1897, 15). Through myth, or as Aristotle puts it by 'undemonstrated belief', Cephalus has 'learned' to be good. Cephalus embodies the simple principles which will be the results of the philosophical adventure of the *Republic*: "the delight of philosophical discourse" over being mastered by desires like the tyrant of Book IX; the recognition of the proper role of material prosperity; and the simple religious belief that a good life is to have been "true in word and deed, and to have paid one's debts to gods and men" (1897, 15–16).

Cephalus came to hold this belief over the course of his not so salutary life, but cannot give an altogether adequate account for his position. As such Oakeshott remarks, follow-

---

[4]   Two principal sources Oakeshott used for his *Republic* notebooks were Richard Lewis Nettleship's Plato Lectures, published in Nettleship's *Philosophical Lectures and Remains* (1897) and Bernard Bosanquet's *Companion to the Republic of Plato* (1906). Richard Lewis Nettleship (1846–1892) was educated at Uppington School, graduating Oxford in 1865 where he studied with T.H. Green (whose lectures he would later prepare for publication along with a memoir of Green) and B. Jowett. Nettleship lectured at Oxford principally on Plato and logic and later edited, with Green and others Lotze's *Logik* and *Metaphysik*, under the editorship of B. Bosanquet. He died in a storm climbing the Swiss Alps (Nettleship 1897, xi–lvi). Bernard Bosanquet (1847–1923) was also a student of Green and Jowett and taught briefly at Oxford (as Fellow of University College from 1870–1881) and later at St. Andrews (1903–1908), but spent a good deal of his life writing and doing social work with the London Ethical Society and the Charity Organization Society (Boucher 1997, xxxiv).

ing both Nettleship and Bosanquet (1897, 15; 1920, 38), Cephalus is emblematic of the fact that "experience anticipates the conclusions of philosophy" (*Rep I*:12). Commenting on the discussion with Cephalus over the value of his wealth, Oakeshott notes that Cephalus recognizes, in a simple (but not complete?) way, that "character is the secret of happiness, not circumstance", and is able to see the logical difference between "*condition* and *cause*" that "anticipates the myth of Book X" (*Rep I*:12). Cephalus understands that wealth is not the cause of happiness but what Aristotle will call a necessary external good for some higher good. A good character, good judgment, is what is needed to put wealth in its proper perspective allowing one to desire it for its use and thus not overestimating its contribution to happiness.

Cephalus is pressed about his beliefs and fails to give a rational account and so he must bequeath the argument to his son Polemarchus. This does not indicate for Oakeshott, however, that what Cephalus knows as a result of his life experience is not genuine knowledge.

There is a strange disjunction between the image we already have of Plato from Oakeshott and the reading Oakeshott has of Socrates' interchange with Cephalus. What is meant by 'experience anticipates the conclusions of philosophy' for Oakeshott? Is the knowledge had in experience genuine knowledge? Is it merely the beginning point to gain further knowledge? Is it not really any kind of knowledge at all and ultimately should be replaced by genuine knowledge? Is it a combination of these, and if so how can they be made compatible?

In an important essay on liberal learning, Oakeshott begins by discussing mind and what it is that makes us capable of reflective, intelligent learning. He says that "Mind is made of perceptions, recognitions, thoughts of all kinds; of emotions, sentiments, affections, deliberations and purposes, and of actions which are responses to what is understood to be going on. It is the author not only of the intelligible world in which a human being lives but also of his self-conscious relationship to that world, a self-consciousness which may rise to the condition of a self-understanding" (*VLL* 19). It could be what Oakeshott is doing with Cephalus is showing that learning takes place in many different ways and that the education Cephalus has had, an education where 'life' is his teacher, puts him in a position to be self-consciousness of his way of life but not have a fully worked out explanation or self-understanding of that way of life. In which case, Oakeshott would be leaning in the direction of interpreting Cephalus along the Socratic lines developed in the previous chapter. That is, Cephalus may be viewed as having gained a knowledge, if late in life, of how to behave well. In a 1951 essay, Oakeshott contends that "The greater part, then — perhaps the most important part — of our political education we acquire haphazardly in finding our way about the natural-artificial world into which we are born, and there is no other way of acquiring it" (*VLL* 152). But, this is not the kind of knowledge of behaving well that Socrates is necessarily after, for a philosophical understanding has little, if any, impact on actually behaving well. The Socrates of the last chapter, recall, is a philosophical radical but also a social conservative. What makes this reading possible is the antecedent recognition that there are qualitatively different kinds of knowledge. In order for Socrates to be able to 'learn' from Cephalus he must have genuine knowledge (knowledge of how to behave), but there must be another kind of knowledge that Cephalus does not have or cannot relay. In the case of Cephalus he has learned by experience and this is genuine knowledge worth knowing about for Socrates. But, it is not philosophical knowledge of good human conduct. It is not satisfying for the philosopher to have *any* reason for behaving well; the philosopher wants to know justice itself and the reason to pursue it for its own sake.

The beginning point of knowledge is the kind of knowledge Cephalus has. Oakeshott remarks of these early exchanges in the dialogue that "this conversation is a kind of *data* for philosophical theory. The healthy moral conscience furnishes the data of ethics" (*Rep* I:12–13). Aside from reflecting the Aristotelian position that a good moral character is the necessary starting point for an ethical study, there is a significant point being made about how philosophy begins. As Oakeshott says in an essay likely published in 1946,

> The starting place in philosophy, then, is not in some remote region of experience known only to the philosopher. Philosophy begins with the concepts of ordinary, everyday knowledge, and consists in an extended, detailed and complete exposition of those concepts, an exposition which is itself a definition.

As such, Oakeshott continues, reformulating Socrates' notion of reminiscence,

> In philosophy, therefore, there is no such thing as a transition from mere ignorance to complete knowledge; the process is always one of coming to know more fully what is in some sense already known (*RPML* 128).

Oakeshott makes note of how the *Republic* begins, how it starts with the common ideas one may have of justice, or with what we might call today cultural assumptions or popular opinion. Oakeshott references many common views of happiness expressed in the early part of the dialogues. He references Herodotus' account of Solon and Croesus (*Rep I*:30–33), Aristotle's point in the *Nicomachean Ethics* about not calling one happy until one is dead (1100a10–14), and Pericles' funeral oration (*Rep I*:12). He makes note of how Cephalus' recollection of the myths told in youth and Pindar's promise of just life (331a) are beginning points, or the date, for political theory (as is, of course, Cephalus' nascent definition of justice as speaking the truth and giving back what is owed).

When this early data is interrogated, however, Cephalus leaves the dialogue. Why? The immediate answer is that Polemarchus breaks into the conversation. Why is he meant to impose himself? Is he protecting his father from Socrates uncovering the shallow reasoning that supports Cephalus' life up to this point? Is it to remove ancestral piety, which Cephalus is said to represent?[5] Oakeshott thinks neither. Remaining more consistent with Oakeshott's overall reading of the *Republic* as a philosophic work, and with Oakeshott's understanding of Socrates as socially conservative,[6] Oakeshott records Nettleship's comment that "Cicero remarks that it would not have been appropriate for Socrates to argue with Cephalus" (*Rep I*:13; 1897, 15). As was remarked earlier, one should heed Aristotle's advice to attend to the unreflective experience of elders; to learn from it, not criticize it. It is genuine knowledge but not the kind of knowledge which can be learned from Cephalus by engaging him in dialectic. Cephalus himself cannot give an account or a *logos* and it would be inappropriate for Socrates to insist on one given Cephalus' advanced years.

---

[5] This is Allan Bloom's reading of this transition (1968, 7n21).
[6] See Chapter 3.

How does one make progress then? What does one do with these data for political theory? Oakeshott notes how the dialectical process of investigation begins once Cephalus leaves the conversation. "Socrates shows that there are circumstances in practical life which fall outside this theory — therefore the theory is not a true one" (*Rep I*:13). The two experiences reveal an incoherence; the description of justice as telling the truth and giving back what is owed is not adequate. What is needed is a definition that encompasses those additional circumstances as well. And so, we get a "modification of [the] definition of justice. 'Suitable for' not 'owed to' [or] 'due'. This allows for varying circumstances" (*Rep I*:13). But, Polemarchus' definition in turn is shown to be defective: as applying only to "action and not disposition", and therefore justice becomes the art of stealing. This conclusion reduces Polemarchus to a state of *aporia*. He is outwitted by a superior dialectician, and this clears the way for "a truer definition" to be built up now that Polemarchus recognizes his helpless ignorance (*Rep I*:14). Polemarchus, the representative of "the present generation", is a "man who has accepted a good tradition but has not understood it" — even at the level that Cephalus may have understood it. "For this reason Socrates can drive him to utter confusion" and when "he at last reaches a point when he is conscious of ignorance (334b)" the "construction begins (334c–336a)" (*Rep I*:10). Polemarchus does not have even the practical knowledge and certitude that comes from life experience of Cephalus and so can easily be driven to confusion.

Oakeshott ends this section dealing with the conversation with Polemarchus by addressing the definition of justice Polemarchus has put forth: justice is helping friends and harming enemies. Oakeshott notes the fundamental importance of the doctrine that the just man never does injury to others (friend or enemy) and references the *Crito* and Socrates' unwillingness to injure the state by defying the laws and escaping (*Rep I*:15). Oakeshott summarizes the progress the dialogue has made up to this point by quoting Bosanquet:

> It has been shown that the respect for property is an inadequate account of righteousness, even in its simple form of honesty; that morality is not mere ability, but that without some ability there cannot be real morality; that personal friendship and enmity are no guides to the right treatment of persons: that goodness

excludes malevolence, not from mere repugnance to giving pain, but from respect for character (*Rep I*:16).

Oakeshott highlights in the margin this point about character. One does not injure another because of some natural pity or sympathy for the pain of others (as Rousseau might argue), or out of 'humanity', but out of respect for character; out of the reasoned belief that acting malevolently toward another is beneath one who has mastery over oneself and over one's lower desires. The argument has moved, to put it slightly differently, from a standpoint of self-interest (doing justice to avoid the penalty) to an enlightened self-interest (where a larger communal good is served by helping friends and harming enemies), to pursuing the good for its own sake (it is in keeping with one's character, and is a kind of self-mastery). Note this is a vast improvement from Cephalus' mere recognition that character is a key to happiness. Through dialogue, this truth has been brought to the floor, a *logos* is beginning to be provided.

In a powerful passage that follows the distinction Oakeshott makes between self-consciousness and self-understanding Oakeshott continues:

> This inherent 'freedom' of a human being lies not only in his ability to make statements expressing his understanding of himself, but also in the world's being for him what he understands it to be, and in his being what he understands himself to be. A human being is 'free', not because he has 'free will', but because his is *in* himself what he is *for* himself (*VLL* 19).

What Oakeshott is saying here in this very Hegelian formulation, and may be working toward in the notebooks in this treatment of Cephalus, is that though Cephalus cannot give a *logos* for why he is behaving the way he is, he has intuitively understood that the higher rationale for acting well resides in remaining true to one's character and not in any utilitarian justification.

This reading (of Cephalus and Socrates) is in sharp contrast to Zeller and is illuminated in the different readings Zeller and Oakeshott give to the use of the *techne* analogies. The analogy of justice to various *technai* could have a number of implications. The force of the analogy is to hem-in activities, to imply a determinate subject matter that can be mastered and taught (Roochnik 1990, 20). This is accomplished both by implying a specific knowledge is involved in any activity and that there is a specified end (*telos*) toward which that knowledge is applied. Oakeshott tends to focus on the former rather than the latter in understanding Socrates' use of *techne* analogies. The use of these metaphors for justice is to point out, following Nettleship, that

> Justice is a power to do something, and so far it is like any art ... In order to live properly we must understand life; according to the saying attributed to Socrates, 'virtue is knowledge,' which really means that to understand life is to be master of it (*Rep I*:15; 1897, 22).

Oakeshott then urges a comparison with Zeller (1868, Chapter 7).

Zeller argues Socrates was a practical moralist in his teaching that virtue is knowledge. Zeller agrees with the reading that to do anything well is to have some knowledge of it, but continues, relying heavily on Xenophon's portrayal of Socrates, to argue that Socrates, in failing to give specificity to what knowledge of the good was, was forced to fall back on custom, ultimately bringing him to "a utilitarian standard" (1868, 123–25). Socrates, Zeller argues, "almost always grounded his moral precepts on the motive of utility".[7] That this reading does gross injustice to the Socrates of the *Apology* who argues that virtue ought to be pursued for its own sake is clear. It is not surprising that Oakeshott omits all of it.

One's environment is a critical element in Oakeshott's understanding of Plato's thinking on education. It is perhaps not surprising that Plato begins, and Oakeshott takes note of this fact, with an education in music, especially lyric poetry sung to music, for the poems of Homer and Hesiod (the 'Bible of Greece') was the repository of many stories told to the

---

[7]   The list of examples Zeller provides, almost wholly from Xenophon, is instructive: "we should aim at being continent, because the continent man has a more pleasant life than the incontinent: we should inure ourselves to hardships, because the hardy man is more healthy, and because he can more easily avoid dangers, and gain honour and glory: we should be modest, because boasting does harm and brings disgrace. We should be on good terms with our relatives, because it is absurd to harm ourselves by those who have been given us for our good; we should try to secure good friends, since a good friend is the most useful possession. We should not withdraw from public affairs, since the well-being of the community is the well-being of the individual; we should obey the laws, since obedience is productive of the greatest good to ourselves and the state; and we should abstain from wrong, since wrong is always punished in the end. In short we should live virtuously, because virtue carries off the greatest rewards both with God and man" (1868, 125–26).

young as moral lessons. In a rather curious reliance on Nettleship, Oakeshott sees that the education in myth and religion is meant to show that

> The greatest thing a man can learn is to see according to man's measure the presence of reason and a divine intelligence in the world about him. So from the earliest stages education is the method of helping the soul see the good, but in all kinds of different ways (1897, 81; *Rep* I:34).

What is interesting about recording this reference is the broad way Oakeshott interprets its meaning. He does not take it to show Plato's belief in divine providence or as an argument from design. Rather, what this reflects is that "At the bottom of Plato's ideas of education etc; is the idea of the responsiveness of the soul. This is a primary necessity. Spiritual Marriage" (*Rep* I:34).

This notion of 'spiritual marriage' must have been significant to Oakeshott for he uses the term at a number of other points.[8] What he has in mind by this spiritual marriage in not immediately clear. Bosanquet commenting on the same passage, where Socrates insists that the beginning is the most important part of education, says that

> Plato's real or working conception of the soul cannot be appreciated apart from his views on education and actual life. Nothing is more characteristic of these views than his insistence on the thorough responsiveness of the soul to the moral, intellectual, and physical environment, including heredity. An abstract or negative spiritualism is fundamentally incompatible with the whole tendency of his thought (1906, 88).

What Oakeshott seems to mean by Plato's notion of a spiritual marriage is two-fold. First, that one's internal mental and spiritual life is deeply affected by one's external conditions. Second, that external conditions and character must be made to harmonize and mutually reinforce one another, hence the long discussion of poetry and its subsequent censorship. The question Plato has before him, according to Oakeshott, is "What is the best literature for drawing out what is best in human nature?" (*Rep* I:40). This is a crucial question for Plato because of the responsiveness of the soul to one's environment. Oakeshott continues, "At the root of all this discussion [of poetry] is Plato's belief that man is essentially an imitative

---

[8]   At *Rep* I:45, I:51, and I:72.

being. What makes men better is the opportunity and ability to imitate that which is really good and noble" (*Rep I*:40v).[9]

Poetry is singled out, not because Plato's thinks "the world can be formed by art alone" (*Rep I*:42v), but, following Nettleship's reading here, Plato's belief and principle is

> that music and every art expresses character ([*ethos*]) in the soul of the man who produces it, and in the soul of the man to whom it appeals. One art differs from another in the medium it uses, but in all there is character, good or bad ([*euetheia* or *kakoetheia*]). No art, therefore, can help being educational; it affects character because it expresses character (*Rep I*:41v; 1897, 108).

It is Plato's logical conclusion that human beings are fundamentally imitative beings, reinforced by Plato's desire to reform Athens, that is the source of Plato's philosophical errors. Plato is often led astray, Oakeshott indicates in his criticism of complexity in music to "propose retrograde movements" (*Rep I*:41). The desire for simple discipline gets the better of Plato's philosophical side. "Plato is a little carried away here [in the discussion of simplicity in music and athletic training] in the application of his principle — as indeed he not seldom is" (*Rep I*:44). Nettleship makes a similar point:

> This is one of the cases [of Plato's craving for discipline and simplicity] where the spirit of the reformer, of which Plato had a good deal in him, does not harmonize with the philosophical temper, and where impatience of what he thinks abuses vitiates his theory (1897, 126).

Oakeshott sees this impatient, reforming zeal to result in a failure on Plato's part to attempt to resolve what Oakeshott

---

[9]   It is interesting to note that Oakeshott brackets this whole treatment of poetry by Plato by indicating that "None of Plato's regulations [on poetry] would in any way limit what is recognized as great in art. Great art would still be far out of their [the guardians'] reach" (*Rep I*:40v). Though Oakeshott gave a good deal of analysis to Plato's aesthetic theory, and read many idealists who had a strong interest in aesthetics, it cannot be doubted that Oakeshott himself did not work out at this point a full-blown aesthetic theory of his own. The publication of *The Voice of Poetry in the Conversation of Mankind* in 1959, and the impulse behind the essay (to retract an ill thought out remark in *Experience and Its Modes*, that poetry was a practical activity), marks Oakeshott's more sustained attempt to work out his own understanding of the character of poetry. Oakeshott did write on poetry in what may have been his dissertation in application for a fellowship at Gonville and Caius College in 1924–1925. In this extended essay titled "An Essay on the Relations of Philosophy, Poetry and Reality" he analyzes poetry and links it to religion and mysticism as a way of apprehending reality in a non-rational way (2004, 67–115).

sees as a tension between two Platonic principles. On the one hand, there is this picture of the soul ("that principle of unity and movement in the body which makes it a living whole" (*Rep I*:43; 1897, 125)) as predominantly imitative. As such, the careful control of one's bodily fitness and one's environment is critical to the educational endeavor: there must be a 'spiritual marriage' — a harmony between internal and external conditions for a human being. However, Plato also insists on the transformative power of knowledge of the 'Good' itself. As Nettleship puts it,

> no line can be drawn between the intellectual and the moral nature; what is called knowledge is not an entirely separate part of the mind unaffected by other parts, and a man cannot be affected by moral evil in one part of his soul and retain intellectual insight into its nature with another part . . . if the character is affected the organ of judgment is affected, because the soul is one and continuous (1897, 128; *Rep I*:45).

In one of the very few instances where Oakeshott poses a question in the notebooks, he asks about the relationship between knowledge (*episteme*) and personal experience (*paradeigmata*), "How relate this to his other doctrine of spiritual marriage?" (*Rep I*:45). To put the question differently, how does one reconcile Plato's claim that the soul is fundamentally imitative, with the claim that beholding the 'good', grasping 'being', revolutionizes both one's understanding of the sensual world and one's moral behavior? Does knowledge consist of seeing and imitating good examples or is it about the turning of the soul toward the good?

It is Oakeshott's attempt to understand the nature of this relationship between experience and knowledge and the attempt to make sense of these two different claims of Plato, that, I argue, results in Oakeshott's particular reading of the Platonic Forms and the 'Good' in Platonic thinking.

The Ideas and the Good

Toward the end of Book V, where the question of truth arises in connection with the claim that the just city can come to being only with the coincidence of power and philosophy, Oakeshott begins his analysis of Platonic 'Ideas' or 'Forms'. The Platonic Ideas are "the elements of unity in the manifold objects or things which we apprehend by the senses" (*Rep*

I:66). This diverges from other readings of the Platonic Forms as 'things' separate from the actual objects of the senses. Bosanquet spends a good deal of time attempting to disabuse people of readings of the Forms that come from sources other than the 'simple' presentation Plato gives of them himself: from "the conceptions which have been derived from Aristotle's account of the doctrine, from clearly mythical passages in Plato himself (as in the myth of the *Phaedrus*), and from vague echoes of Kantian 'things-in-themselves'" (1906, 206).

Earlier in the notebook (*Rep I*:38v), Oakeshott comments on the passage where Socrates is analyzing and redefining the traditional Greek virtues to point out how Plato saw the interconnectedness of these virtues. Oakeshott records Nettleship's comment that

> It is characteristic of Plato to be perpetually showing, as he does in this passage, points of connection between things apparently different; his conceptions are never at rest in his hands, but are continually passing into each other (1892, 96; *Rep I*:38v).

And, Oakeshott notes

> All this shows that Plato lived his philosophy. When he spoke his words were but the overflowing of his inner life. It was not so much a power of memory which kept all things connected but the fact that they formed a single whole in his life — a whole which he was rehearsing with himself (*Rep I*:38v).

What is interesting about this comment about Plato's dynamic mind and the lively connection between the Plato's internal and external world is a reference to Aristotle.

Oakeshott urges a comparison with Aristotle's characterization of Plato in the *Nicomachean Ethics*, which directly ties Oakeshott's comment to his understanding of the Platonic Forms. Here Aristotle is taking exception to Plato's Forms as in any way relevant to ethics and action (1196b35). Oakeshott also references Stewart's note on this passage in Aristotle.[10] Stewart says that Aristotle

> Seems to regard the Idea as an object of the speculative reason alone, something as metaphysical and standing apart; and between the speculative and practical powers of man he sets a gulf. Plato, on the other hand, speaking without this analytical clearness, seems to think that the Idea as an object for the imagina-

---

[10]   Oakeshott relied heavily in the notebooks on Aristotle's *Ethics* on J.A. Stewart's *Notes on the Nichomachean Ethics of Aristotle*, Two Vol. (1892). References to this commentary will be by volume and page number.

tion, as well as the reason, as being an ideal as well as an idea. In this its many-sided character he would make it affect life as well as knowledge; for by contemplation of it the mind would become conformed to it (1892, I:89).

Stewart seems to equivocate a bit on this point in this passage. What does he mean by indicating that the Form is the ideal and the idea? Why does this not presume the Form is something separate from any particular experience? Aristotle's critique of Plato's Forms and Plato's presentation of the Forms must have remained a strong interest for Stewart for he developed this argument that the 'Ideas' are not things separate in themselves in his book *Plato's Doctrine of Ideas* (1909). This was a source, as we shall see, that had a strong impact on Oakeshott's understanding of the Platonic Forms.[11]

Stewart argues that Plato's doctrine of ideas expresses a 'double' experience of Plato:

> it was the Experience of one keenly interested in, and highly capable of taking, the scientific point of view in all departments of knowledge; and it was also the Experience of one singularly sensitive to aesthetic influences. It was the Experience of one who was a great man of science and connoisseur of scientific method, and also a great artist (1909, 3).

It is Plato the scientist *and* the poet that accounts, according to Stewart, for the often confusing language Plato uses to discuss the Forms. So, Stewart separates two different doctrines of the Forms: one that expresses Plato's scientific understanding of the Forms and how the Forms underpin his methodological approach; and another that expresses an aesthetic experience of the Forms.

Oakeshott is clearly struck by the argument for he makes great use of Stewart's book toward the end of the second *Republic* notebook.[12] "The object of scientific thought is the

---

[11] Oakeshott's interest in this line of argument must have remained with him, for he uses an identical phrase in the LSE Lecturers. Oakeshott says of the first lecture on Plato, it will be on Plato's intellectual apparatus or "what the books call 'Plato's doctrine of Ideas'" (*LSE* 132). Oakeshott then proceeds to argue that Plato's use of idea is much more akin to the contemporary use of essence, or a necessary quality of a thing rather than its accidental, circumstantial or contingent ones (*LSE* 133).

[12] Oakeshott devotes ten pages in the notebook to brief interpretative remarks on a series of Platonic dialogues, relying heavily on Stewart's argument (*Rep II*:27–36). Oakeshott provides a citation to Stewart's book explicitly at the start of these pages, and indicates special attention should be paid to pages 119–127

[*eidos*]. The [*eidos*] is 'the scientific point of view' — not, as Aristotle thought, as separate things. . . . Socrates refuses to speak of the Good as a 'thing'" (*Rep II*:32). The language here that Oakeshott uses in the notebooks is Stewart's. As Stewart puts the doctrine of ideas:

> The Ideas, so far as their methodological significance is concerned, are nothing more than concepts-in-use — the instruments by employing which Human Understanding performs its work of interpreting the world — this sensible world, not another world beyond. This view of the function of Ideas in science Plato holds and enforces throughout the whole series of his Dialogues, and nowhere more plainly than in his earliest Dialogues, where the Moral Virtues by exhibiting each in its special context — by assigning to each a special place and use in the Social System, the System of the 'Good' (1909, 6–7).

It is noteworthy that Oakeshott makes reference to Socrates here and that Stewart indicates it is the early (what Oakeshott classed the more 'Socratic dialogues') dialogues that show this understanding of the ideas clearly. The picture of the Ideas here is not of a separate reality that lies outside sensuous experience and which is a replacement for the defective reality our senses present us (a picture one is inclined to from Oakeshott's published interpretation of Plato). Rather, the description is more like searching or hunting for *in experience* a common or essential quality of some thing (be it justice, or virtue, or love) among all that accompanies it. One might go so far as to say that the former is a correspondence theory of truth and the latter a coherence theory of truth. Be that as it may, there is more to say about the process of seeking knowledge and the kind of knowledge that is had.

The search for knowledge is more than finding the *eidos* on either of these readings of the Forms. Plato, whether understood as arguing for a transcendent reality behind our sensuous experience that is beheld through philosophic contemplation or an immanent reality to be sought in the confusion of goings-on that make up our experience, insists on unity and system. That is, it is not enough to know that justice is 'minding one's own business', the meaning of this definition is only realized if understood as part of a larger complex of interrelated meanings. This justice has meaning only as part of

---

(where Stewart forcefully argues that Aristotle's critique is more applicable to later Platonists, and that Plato's Ideas are not separate things-in-themselves).

a system of virtues, each of which have their necessary place.[13] To understand any particular virtue is to understand its essential quality in relation to its place in a larger system (of essential qualities). It is striking just how similar Stewart's description of the Ideas mirrors Oakeshott own description of the aims of philosophical activity in his later published work. Compare the following passages:

> The [*eidos*], then, of Courage or Temperance is the whole setting of the quality so named — its *context*. To fill in context is the problem of science; and if we say that the discovery of the [*eidos*], or [*idea*], the *inventio formae*, in any inquiry, is the 'adequate filling in of context round about the object of inquiry', we are using the phrase which perhaps covers the ground better than any other (1909, 120).

> All explanation, all interpretation, may be seen as a matter of deciding upon and examining the appropriate setting for what is to be explained and of exhibiting it in its place in that setting. Given a 'text', something partially disconnected, obscure, imperfectly conceived, explanation is the attempt to find the 'context' and to relate text and context so that they become a single whole (*CPJ* 350).

The former is Stewart, the latter is Oakeshott in an often overlooked essay written in 1938.[14] Or again, consider another of Stewart's characterizations of the Ideas:

> 'Separate' does not mean 'separate' as one *Thing* is from another Thing, as one *Person* is from another Person. It means 'abstract'; and when the [*eidos*] is said to be 'separate' from the particular, the meaning is that, on the one hand, you have the particular Thing, or Event, or Quality, or Quantity, here and now presented to sense — a concrete phenomena here and now, but abstract — and *explanation*, in short, not a *phenomena to be explained* — an explanation which *always* holds good (1909, 125).

---

[13] In a combination of Socratic playfulness and methodological exposition, Socrates hunts for the cardinal virtues and once all, save justice, are found what remains must necessarily be justice (428a). Oakeshott is so taken by the images of 'Socratic method' as they are depicted here and earlier that he records and cross-references them in his notebook (*Rep* I:40, 54). The image of the hunt (432b) and the earlier image of following the argument as if a wind may take us (394d) are, quoting Bosanquet "beautiful expression[s] of the dialectic method in all its faith and freedom" (*Rep* I:40; 1906:98).

[14] This essay, "The Concept of a Philosophical Jurisprudence", has many similarities to a later essay (written around 1946) titled "The Concept of a Philosophy of Politics" (*RPML* 119–137).

This description fits remarkably well the way Oakeshott characterized the procedure Socrates used in the early discussion, above, of justice in the *Republic*. And, this description strongly resembles the understanding Oakeshott persistently had of the activity of philosophy and the activity of understanding more generally. Compare, for example the following description of the attempt to understand philosophically:

> The aim of philosophy is to arrive at concepts which, because they presuppose nothing, are complete in themselves; the aim is to define and establish concepts so fully and so completely that nothing remains to be added. Definition is a matter of degree. All thinking is the attempt to define concepts, and philosophy is merely what occurs when thought is allowed to follow its own bent with unqualified freedom. Thought, the character of which is exemplified in every attempt at intellectual comprehension, is perfectly exemplified in philosophical comprehension (*CPJ* 345).

The way Oakeshott, then, understands the Platonic Ideas is as concepts, the philosophical use of which is always the attempt to further define their meaning—a meaning which is only clearly articulated when set in the larger context from which it is abstracted.

In the abstract metaphysical and epistemological dialectic that Socrates takes Glaucon through over opinion and knowledge, Oakeshott makes few but very pregnant points about the Platonic Forms that further support this understanding. The upshot is to further pinpoint the object of philosophic knowledge, which is to find the truth, the Form, the essence, or the 'nature' of a thing. But, as we have seen, the Form of a thing is not a thing itself, but an aspect of a thing. "To state Plato's conception of the philosophic mind briefly, it is one which constantly looks for principles or laws or unities of which the manifold of our experience is the phenomena" (*Rep I*:67v; 1897, 195). The Form is not understood as a rigid thing independent of and existing apart from concrete experience.

Oakeshott is tracing a line between Plato as advocate of a correspondence theory of truth on the one hand and the relativity of Protagoras' "man is the measure" on the other. "Opinions' objects are all relative. A beautiful thing in other circumstances may be ugly—and so on. It is no more true to say that it is beautiful than it is ugly. But philosophic natures always look for the unity in these manifold beauties and not-beauties" (*Rep I*:67). One must search out in experience itself the elements of permanence.[15]

Before saying a word about the other part of Stewart's argument on the Ideas as they relate to aesthetic experience, it is worthwhile noting here that Oakeshott is following a more Socratic understanding of the Ideas than a Platonic one, and that in the end, as I argue below, this difference results in very different understandings of the philosophical study of politics.

It is worthwhile to notice as well how the earlier metaphysical quarrels among the pre-Socratics figure into the argument here. Without stretching the point too far, one could say that Parmenidian metaphysics, that what is is and doesn't change and what does change is illusion and not reality, fits well with the aspect of Plato that adheres to a correspondence theory of truth. And, this opens him up not only to Aristotle's charge of being abstract, but also to the charges of otherworldliness, esotericism, etc. Heraklitian metaphysics, of seeing the unchanging principle in all the changes, dovetails more with a Socratic/Oakeshottian search for the unity in our sensuous world of experience.[16]

For Oakeshott, as we have seen, the concept or the idea emanates from a particular practice, rather than the practice being a reflection or copy of some abstract Idea or Form. How one comes to know the idea is not where Oakeshott and Plato differ. Oakeshott indicates in the preface to his analysis of the cave allegory in *On Human Conduct*, that "this account of the engagement of understanding owes so much to the account of Plato (*Republic*, vi, *ad init.* and elsewhere)" (*OHC* 27). What is more instructive is where Oakeshott diverges. Two dominant differences are already clear. One, which we have already

---

[15] Oakeshott references Zeller on Socrates at this point: "Socrates taught his followers to acquire knowledge by dealing with notions critically" (*Rep I*:67). What is interesting is how Oakeshott reads Plato here and that he omits what immediately follows in Zeller: that "Plato concluded at once that objective conceptions were alone real, in any true sense, and that consequently only a derivative reality belonged to other things . . . Lastly, Aristotle arrived at the conclusion that conceptions are in things, constituting their real essence and cause of motion" (1868, 43). Oakeshott clearly reads Plato in a more Socratic and Aristotelian manner, abstracting the Forms less than Zeller has Plato doing. Though, one should note, Oakeshott does not as a result embrace Aristotle's teleology.

[16] One might also usefully compare the Hobbesian metaphysic of matter in motion.

seen, is that the philosopher upon reentering the cave is depicted by Plato as having a knowledge superior to those still bound in the cave and that this knowledge is of a character that it can substitute for the knowledge the cave-dwellers have of how to conduct their affairs. The second significant difference is equally important and is a condition of the first.

The difference here is that Plato presupposes the cosmos to be permeated with an almost mystical order, where every particular going-on is a reflection of that underlying natural order. This belief takes vivid expression in the Myth of Er at the end of the *Republic* and is intimated in the separation between the sensual realm of *doxa* and the intelligible realm of *episteme* and in the notion of the 'Good' as a system. Though Oakeshott is not abandoning the idea that there is coherence in the world, he is clear that the coherence that exists does not derive from the same source as, at least one side of, Plato assumes. A puzzle remains, however. How does one account for all of the language in Plato about the being of the beautiful and the beholding of the 'Good'. For Plato nature is the source, for Oakeshott human beings themselves are the source. For this we need to return to Stewart's argument.

Stewart distinguishes the presentation of Plato's doctrine of ideas as a scientific methodology from the aesthetic treatment of the ideas. What Stewart is arguing is that the ideas and the system of ideas that emerges from this philosophical activity are capable of being experienced in a way other than philosophically. In the scientific or philosophical way

> The question always is: By employing what principles, and following what method, does Human Understanding succeed in explaining the facts of sensible experience? And the answer is: By bringing its logical categories to bear upon the facts of sensible experience, and so thinking out systematically the various contexts, first immediate, and then wider and wider, in which alone these facts have any significance for conduct or science (1909, 128).

Alternatively, the system of ideas that results from the philosophic activity is capable of being, not interrogated further to seek more specification and coherence, but looked at *as* a thing. A philosophic system or idea may be

> merely gazed at for the sake of its own individuality; it is an end in itself, not a means to something else; it is not a product of anything which went before; it is not the cause or sign of anything to come.

> This is what something familiar, or beautiful, always is to one
> whom it fills with love or wonder (Stewart 1909, 132).

That is to say, a philosophic system is capable of being contemplated aesthetically.[17] Stewart argues that Plato's language in describing the contemplation of philosophic images accounts for the misunderstanding of Plato's doctrine of ideas as separate things-in-themselves. It was, then, Plato's strong poetic disposition that led him to speak of the ideas as separate *sensibilia*, but in discussing them philosophically and as a method of education, he never failed to distinguish the poetic experience of the Ideas from the philosophical use of the Forms according to Stewart.[18]

The notebooks reveal, then, a rather peculiar and sympathetic reading of Plato—a much more sympathetic reading than later published accounts would indicate. The reading is achieved by positing two sides to Plato. The Socratic side of Plato (isolated in part by Stewart's argument about Plato the philosopher and Plato the poet) is interested in philosophical explanation and description and not interested in social change per se. The reforming Plato is the one who formulates the doctrine of ideas as part of a separate, superior realm of knowledge and reality, a reality that is released from the contingency of our everyday opinions and is suited as a complete substitute for our mistaken knowledge. The Socratic side of Plato, though not abandoning the belief that this knowledge is superior to cave knowledge, differs on three fundamental points. First, through Cephalus, Socrates understands a genuine kind of knowledge that the cave dwellers have. Second, the knowledge that is had out of the cave is not a completely separate knowledge from, and a substitute for, cave dwellers' knowledge. Instead, and third, philosophical knowledge is a

---

[17] One cannot help but recall a brief essay Oakeshott wrote on Hobbes's *Leviathan*, where he suggests that *Leviathan* is more susceptible than many other practical and philosophical reflections on politics to being understood from a poetic standpoint. "It's effect is an expansion of our faculty of dreaming. Under its inspiration the familiar outlines of the common dream fade, new perceptions, and emotions hitherto unfelt, are excited within us, the till-now settled fact dissolves once more into infinite possibility, and we become aware that the myth (which is the substance of the dream) has acquired a new quality, without our needing to detect the precise character of the change" (1947, 966).

[18] This reading may account for that curious footnote in the *Voice of Poetry* essay mentioned earlier where Oakehsott notes Plato misidentified philosophical experience (*RIP* 516n13).

rational articulation of what is only partially known and immanent in the cave.

The dual disposition Oakeshott sees in Plato is powerfully played out in Oakeshott's and Plato's understanding of the state. The similarities and differences in how Plato and Oakeshott approach the state further advances Oakeshott's story of the refinement of the philosophical activity and shows how Platonic thinking about the state (with both its advances and its mistakes) is alive today.

Chapter V

Plato, Oakeshott, and the State

Oakeshott shared with Plato the belief that the political regime is a reflection of the moral character of the associates that make up the regime. It is this belief and the idealism it implies that underpins both Platonic and Oakeshottian thinking.[1] Plato's idealism, however, mixes a disposition to be philosophical about the regime with a disposition to reform the regime. We saw in the last chapter how this impacted Oakeshott's evaluation of Platonic philosophy. Equally it is a part of Oakeshott's treatment of Plato on the state. One might say the philosophical mistakes Plato made that were identified in the last chapter account for Oakeshott's criticism of the Platonic state and for only a partial, but important, adoption of Plato's theoretical treatment of the relationship of the individual to the state. Plato's disposition to be both philosopher and reformer has an analogue in the way Oakeshott describes the dual disposition of the associates in the modern European state, and points out the continuing relevance of Platonic thought and Oakeshott's reformulation and critique of it.

Beginning to Theorize the State

There is a powerful congruence between Oakeshott and Plato in their presuppositions about how to theorize the state. Or, more properly, there is a congruence between Oakeshott's

---

[1] This belief is not only important in understanding the state but powerfully contributes to the importance of education for Plato and Oakeshott. If the political regime is a reflection of the dispositions of the associates, meaningful changes in the regime come, not from a rearrangement of institutions but from the changes in the self-understanding of individuals.

assumptions and his understanding of Plato's assumptions. Oakeshott's reading of Plato on the state is, like his reading of Hobbes, not the orthodox reading.

In Oakeshott's notes on the *Republic* he records a passage from Nettleship's set of Plato lectures in which Plato theorizes the state. Nettleship places great emphasis on the method-ological path Socrates advances in the search for justice in Book II. Socrates suggests it might be better to look for justice in the city, which is larger, and once found it will more easily be detected in the soul, which is smaller (368d). This is a criti-cal turning point in the argument for Nettleship: "To under-stand the import of this transition is to understand the principle of the whole argument of the *Republic*" (1897, 67; *Rep I*:29). That principle is not any of the usual suspects: that phi-losophers should rule, or that everyone has a distinguishable role to play in the natural, hierarchical organism that is society, or that democracy rules by opinion and not by wisdom or knowledge. Rather,

> The whole of the *Republic* is really an attempt to interpret human nature psychologically; the postulate upon which its method rests is that all the institutions of society, class organization, law, religion, art and so on, are ultimately products of the human soul, an inner principle of life which works itself out in these outward shapes . . . Plato's position is that the life of the state is the life of the men composing it, as manifested in a way comparatively easy to observe . . . The 'justice of the state', then, is the justice of the indi-viduals who compose it . . . We must bear in mind throughout Plato's argument that there is no state apart from the individual men and women who compose it (1897, 68–69; *Rep I*:29).

What is central to understand, for Oakeshott (and Oakeshott sees this as the preeminent occupation of Plato in the *Republic*), is the nature or the character of the individuals who compose the state.[2] Oakeshott and Plato may diverge, as we shall see, on the character of these individuals, but what should be noticed here is the idealism that this view implies

---

[2]   For Plato what is necessary in order to understand the state is an understand-ing of the structure of the soul. Oakeshott's *On Human Conduct* structurally reflects a similar position. The first essay is devoted to analyzing what it means to theorize human conduct. As a necessary part of this investigation Oakeshott analyzes the character of human beings in such a way that some inquiries are not appropriate (human beings are 'reflective intelligences' and not say machines or processes). Only after understanding human beings and their conduct does Oakeshott turn, in the second and third essays, to theorize the state and the historic fortunes of the modern European state.

which drew Oakeshott and a host of other British Idealists to Plato.

Early British Idealists drew their inspiration from a rediscovery of Plato, from a reaction to what was perceived as the sensationalism and materialism of Hobbes, and from Berkeley long before Hegel made his way across the channel.[3] But, for later Idealists, like Bosanquet and Oakeshott, Hegel becomes a window through which Plato can be understood and interpreted. Oakeshott records in his notebook the following passage from Hegel's *History of Philosophy*:

> If we thus regard the content of the Platonic idea (*i.e.* looking below the surface of life to see whether its fundamental facts are grasped), we shall find that Plato did in fact represent the Greek moral system (*Sittlichkeit*) substantially as what it was; for Greek civil life is what forms the substantial basis of Plato's *Republic*. Plato is not the man to worry himself with abstract theories and principles; his true intelligence has grasped and represented real truth, and this could be nothing else than the truth in which he lived, of that one mind which came to life in him no less than in Greece (*Rep* I:3).[4]

What this passage and the earlier quotation from Nettleship capture is the notion that Platonic philosophy is the attempt to describe the whole of existence, experience, or reality (the truth that Plato lived) by giving a reasoned account of the identity of that reality in all its particulars. One might recall this is how Oakeshott described the aims of philosophy, and how he understood Plato's philosophical aims (at least the more Socratic strain in Plato).

The place to begin in seeking the reality and truth is the thoughts and beliefs of individuals who lived at the time. It is not just the historical conditions but the meanings individuals placed on those goings-on that make up the historical conditions. As Oakeshott puts it in the first essay in *On Human Conduct* an agent "is what he understands [or misunderstands] himself to be, his contingent situations are what he understands [or misunderstands] them to be" (1975, 41). One might recognize this as one of the fundamental postulates Oakeshott relies upon to theorize the state and human conduct, and he

---

[3] See, for example, Muirhead (1992, 14).
[4] This passage is included in Bosanquet's *Companion to Plato's Republic* as part of a series of passages Bosanquet says students of Plato would do well to consider (1906, 16–17). Oakeshott relied heavily on Bosanquet's *Companion* in his notebook.

explicitly draws attention to this postulate again in the third essay (*OHC* 235). The immediate significance consists of two important points.

First, the locus of one's philosophical attention, in understanding the state or any other topic, should be squarely on the self-understanding of the individuals who compose the state, or on what we generally call today the political 'culture'. Though at times Oakeshott may seem to suggest it is the actual activities of government and the great expansion of the power available to modern government are the significant factors in determining the character of the modern European state,[5] he is quite clear the primary source of the character of the state derives from the associates themselves.

> For, although the character of an association, that of the office of government (if any), and that of the associates are conditionally interrelated, each implying the others, it is the third which constitutes the *causa foederis*; and an associate is what he understands himself to be (*OHC* 234).

Second, and closely related, this belief is a fundamental postulate of idealist thinking more generally. Historical and material conditions are important but cannot be separated from the meaning human beings have placed on those historical and material conditions. In this sense, ideas and meanings are primary. Oakeshott insists the world is a world wholly composed of meanings.

> The components of this world are not abstractions ('physical objects') but beliefs. It is a world of facts, not 'things'; of 'expressions' which have meanings and require to be understood because they are the 'expressions' of human minds (*VLL* 45).

One's thoughts or ideas are the source of what gives a unity to reality.

Thinking, in large measure, is an attempt to make more sense of one's reality. To follow the impulse of all thinking without reserve (i.e., philosophical thinking) is the attempt to capture the whole of existence, experience, or reality in thought. In short, philosophy is an attempt to achieve a concrete universal, a coherent map of the totality of experience

---

[5]   For example, he suggests that the number of individual *manqué* are "proportionately greater then ever before, mainly because of the policies of governments" (*OHC* 276).

that does not abstract from particulars but subsumes them in a monistic whole.

Divergence in Idealism

This understanding idealists hold, that reality is a complete and coherent whole (a unity in diversity, a many in one, or an absolute or concrete universal), may lead in two different directions, one more practical and the other more philosophical. That there is a relationship between the philosophical doctrine or explanation and the concrete particulars may suggest not just a philosophical approach but a practical link *from* theory *to* practice (a position we have seen Oakeshott through his reading of Socrates to have rejected).

As David Boucher has pointed out, for the British Idealists,

> with a few exceptions, notably Bradley and McTaggart,[6] philosophy was integrally related to practical life and needed to be directed to improve the condition of society. They maintained that everything in experience was related to everything else. There could be no isolated individuals or facts.

As such,

> Idealism was able to provide a rational basis for belief which, together with its emphasis on the unity and development of human potential, provided a philosophical basis for social legislation.

So strong a basis in fact that

> British idealists were almost evangelical in their reforming zeal and say their position as professional philosophers carried with it a social responsibility to identify and articulate the sources of injustice and depravity, and campaign for reform (Boucher 1997, ix-xi).

Oakeshott did not follow the route of these many British Idealists, including Bosanquet whom he heavily relied upon in his notebooks.

What is striking about Oakeshott's early thinking on Plato's idealism is just how sensitive it is to the varieties of idealism embodied in Plato's thinking. At a critical point in the discus-

---

[6] These two were strong influences on Oakeshott. Oakeshott acknowledged a clear debt to Bradley in the introduction to his *Experience and Its Modes* (1933, 6), and McTaggart first introduced Oakeshott to philosophy as a student at Cambridge (Grant 1990, 13). One might include Oakeshott among these eccentric British Idealists.

sion of the Good in the *Republic*, Oakeshott references McTaggart's essay on "The Necessity of Dogma". He is impressed with McTaggart's argument that "Nothing is true merely because it is good. Nothing is good merely because it is true" (1895, 150). Oakeshott understands Plato, however, to hold the "idea of *knowledge* at the bottom of all goodness. Truth at the bottom of the Good" (*Rep I*:68v). McTaggart makes a clear distinction between truth and goodness, and argues questions of truth and questions of goodness are "independent and ultimate"; that the difficult duty of a thinker "is to avoid confusing the two great questions: Is this real? and Would this be good?" (1895, 150; 1934, 64-65). Oakeshott, as we have seen in the previous chapters, is concerned to avoid collapsing questions of good into questions of truth.

Mystical Monism

This is not the only concern Oakeshott had about Plato's idealism. He also worried about the mysticism implied in the monism of Plato's idealism. In one of the rare moments in the notebooks on the ancient Greeks, Oakeshott poses a question. "Is 'justice' ever attained in other than a mystic state?" referencing McTaggart's essays "Mysticism" and "The Necessity of Dogma" (*Rep I*:57v). Mysticism, McTaggart argues "asserts a greater unity in the universe than that which is recognized in ordinary experience, or in science" and goes on to note that there are two different kinds of unity that may be imagined (1934, 47). "The unity may be regarded as only one aspect of the universe, and as combined with diversity. Or it may be said that, in reality, there is no diversity at all, but only unity" (1934, 50).

There are then at least two separate questions about Plato's idealism that Oakeshott is concerned with at the early stage in his thinking. The one is that Plato collapses questions of goodness and questions of truth into each other. The other is how to account for the unity (and thus the diversity) in experience. Oakeshott is keen in addressing the latter question to insulate Plato from the charge he is an enthusiastic mystic hoping for a release from every element of contingency. So, Oakeshott is careful to follow Bosanquet's translation of the passage where Socrates discusses the magnanimity of the philosopher. "To an understanding endowed with magnificence and the contemplation of all time and all being, do you think it possible",

Socrates asks, "that human life seem anything great?" (486a). Oakeshott remarks on this passage that there is "no thought here of 'another' life or world" (*Rep I:*68). Bosanquet remarks that these passages should be handled carefully "to avoid quietism" (1906, 220). Oakeshott suggests one not understand Plato to be arguing that there exists a mystical unity, the beholding of which annihilates the individual.

Recall how Oakeshott had treated the Platonic Forms. His treatment largely frees Plato from this mysticism, and, interestingly, also from a correspondence theory of truth, especially when read through Stewart's reading of the doctrine of ideas. The Platonic Forms are "the elements of unity in the manifold objects or things which we apprehend by the senses" (*Rep I:*66). It is interesting that McTaggart is evoked here for McTaggart is often thought of as the idealist that merely posits a mystical unity of love, where things like time and space, because they are contradictory, are not real (Robbins 1982, 88).[7] But, though severing the absolute more fully from ordinary experience than Oakeshott does, McTaggart was rather sober about the question of politics, and his sobriety made him a more individualist type of idealist. Unlike Green or Bosanquet, where the individual is far less significant than the unity which was the social whole, McTaggart argued

> each of us is more than the society which unites us, because there is in each of us the longing for perfection which society can never realize. The parts of a living body can find their end in that body, though it is imperfect and transitory. But a man can dream of perfection and, having once done so, he will find no end short of perfection. Here he has no abiding city (Robbins 1988, 88).[8]

One might read both McTaggart's and Bradley's projects in these arguments, about the non-existence of time, to point out the logical contradictions in order to transcend them or to point out the limits of reason to ever come to a perfect logical unity, or both.[9]

At a minimum Oakeshott's notes on these passages clearly show Oakeshott himself was aware of and sensitive to an ide-

---

[7] One might recall Bradley here as well who argued in *Appearance and Reality* that space, time, motion, change, and causation are contradictory and therefore relegated to the realm of appearance rather than reality (1897, 30–52).

[8] The passage is from McTaggart's *Studies in Hegelian Cosmology* (1901, 193), quoted in Robbins (1988).

[9] One might note how the paradoxes of Zeno perform a similar task.

alism that is less absolute than some mystical, monistic absolutism. That there is a unity does not deny that the diversity is real. The earlier question of truth and goodness in Plato's idealism also is instructive, for Oakeshott is most critical of Plato for his practical bent that the mingling of the two implies.

Truth and Goodness

Oakeshott's overall evaluation of Plato and his thinking can only be characterized as one of critical ambivalence. Oakeshott admired Plato's philosophical acumen and generally his understanding of the practice of philosophy and theorizing (*OHC* 27). Oakeshott sees the *Republic* as a masterpiece of moral philosophy. However, and this aspect never ceases to provide occasions for comment by Oakeshott, the *Republic* is also "a book of a *reformer*" (*Rep* I:1). This evaluation of Plato as both philosopher *and* reformer was an enduring one for Oakeshott and he believed it was the zeal of the latter that compromised the former. This evaluation shows up in Oakeshott's first course of lectures at Cambridge given in 1928-29. He praises Plato for his response to the Sophists and their abstract thinking, reading Plato to be urging the Sophists to "think more concretely; have done with abstract divisions like this of nature and convention. If you want to see the life of man truly you must see it as a single whole" (*CL* VIII:3). Echoing Hegel's critique of Plato, which Oakeshott references later in his notebooks (*Rep* I:49), Oakeshott criticizes Plato in the Cambridge lectures for not being idealist enough. Plato still "speaks the language of morality—goodness, justice, what *ought* we to do?" (*CL* VIII:3).

Oakeshott clearly sees the practical thrust of Plato's reflections on politics and the *polis*. Specifically Oakeshott identifies Plato with the political aim to "awaken Athens to her desperate need of discipline". "Sparta he saw", Oakeshott continues, "took life seriously, was scientifically organized–for a purpose—war . . . Athens must be disciplined, scientifically organized for the purpose of 'the good life'" (*Rep* I:4v). A primary event that animated Plato's philosophy, as many others have observed, was the death of Socrates and more particularly how the trial and death of Socrates underscores the "errors of

Athenian democracy".[10] Oakeshott even places him within a political movement "whose chief work was the criticism of the great fifth Century and its statesman".[11]

What is striking is the juxtaposition of this belief that Plato's philosophy is an attempt to correct Athenian democracy with Hegel's famous passage Oakeshott immediately quotes in his notebook from *The Philosophy of Right*:

> It is only when the actual world has reached its full fruition that the ideal rises to confront reality, and builds up, in the shape of an intellectual realm, that same world grasped in its substantial being. When philosophy paints its grey in grey, some one shape of life had meantime grown old: and grey in grey, though it brings it into knowledge, cannot make it young again. The owl of Minerva does not start upon its flight until the evening twilight begins to fall.

The force of Hegel's thought, of course, leans strongly against philosophy being prescriptive and rather toward philosophy's central activities being descriptive and explanatory, a belief Oakeshott never abandoned in his published or unpublished works.

Where Plato is being more philosophical (one might say Socratic) Oakeshott incorporates important insights about the state, and where Plato is wearing his hat as a reformer Oakeshott is critical. It is Plato's reforming zeal that Oakeshott believes distracts him from penetrating further than he does in philosophically working through the idea of the *polis*.

As indicated earlier, one of the criticisms Oakeshott had of Plato was that he didn't go far enough, and I want to pause a moment to notice what Oakeshott might mean by this. First, it should be noticed that Plato *did* go far to begin with, but far in what sense? Oakeshott's notes on Socrates help point the way. Oakeshott sees Socrates' response to the Sophists as significant in that it superceded the distinction between nature and convention. Socrates saw that what human beings *do* is a reflection of what they naturally *are*, so activities like living together and writing laws (conventions) is natural to human beings. Self-consciously making things (artifacts), whether a sculpture or a city with laws, is natural to human beings. As

---

[10]　Oakeshott makes this point in his introduction to *Leviathan* (*RIP* 226).

[11]　He immediately references Pericles and his death in 429 B.C. and references the *Gorgias* 515e & 519a, as well as Hegel's evaluation that "this marks the beginning of decadence (cf. Hegel, Phil d. Rechts. P. 20)" (*Rep I*: 2).

Oakeshott puts it echoing Aristotle, "Man's nature issues in all that he does" (*Rep I*:25v). And, despite whether one believes there is a final cause or *telos* for human beings or the state, and regardless of the Greek understanding of fate, this belief is a central insight of Socrates that Oakeshott believed Plato largely internalized.

However, this Socratic insight is not taken to its logical conclusion, is not pressed far enough philosophically. Oakeshott records Hegel's criticism of Plato on this point from the *History of Philosophy*:

> People set it down as his defect that he was too ideal, but his defect lies rather in this, *that he was not ideal enough.* For if reason is the universal power, and this is essentially intellectual; then as intellectual it involves subjective freedom, which had dawned on the world in Socrates as a new principle. Therefore, though rationality ought to be the basis of law, and is so in the world, yet on the other side it essentially involves conscience, private conviction, in short, all forms of subjective freedom . . . This element in general, this movement of the individual, this principle of subjective freedom, is in Plato in part disregarded, in part purposely violated, because it displayed itself as that which brought about the ruin of Greece (*Rep I*:49).[12]

It is Plato's diagnosis and recommended treatment of Athens' ailment that leads his philosophical thinking in the wrong direction and toward advancing an ideal city that removes elements of diversity and to the purging of the city of all that distracts from its overall unity (what Oakeshott periodically refers to in his notebooks as Plato's monasticism). Interestingly, it is the Socratic side of Plato that gets pushed out. In Oakeshott's LSE lectures on the Roman political experience he mentions that the Roman notions of legality had very few counterparts in the Greek world, but in a handwritten bit of marginalia he references for comparison Plato's dialogue *Crito* (Oakeshott 1960c, 244).[13] Is Oakeshott suggesting that Socrates, despite the great barrier that the Greek moral view presented,[14] was able to grasp the outlines of law as having

---

[12]   Here, as elsewhere, Oakeshott drew the citation from Bosanquet's *Companion* (1906).

[13]   This was a handwritten marginal note and so does not appear in the published volume of his lectures (*LSE* 2006), but only in the original set of lecture notes (1960c).

[14]   The Greek moral view was no doubt deeply impacted by its almost continual belligerence with its neighbors, a condition Oakeshott insists is alien to civil

procedural authority? Perhaps, but what is clear is that Socrates is, for Oakeshott, the representative of the "sceptical, enquiring, spirit" and the "representative of the true philosophical spirit" (*Rep I*:10). Plato, on the other hand, while reflecting this debt to Socrates especially in the early dialogues desired more of a system. Knowledge of the Good, for Plato, "is a science, a system: it can be taught — true education. The raison d'etre of the State", Oakeshott notes (*Rep I*:6).[15]

Individual and State

This invoking of Hegel's critique of Plato serves to draw attention to another Platonic theme in Oakeshott's thinking about the relationship of the individual to the state, and, at the same time the major difference between Plato's thinking about the *polis* and the modern understanding of the state. Oakeshott views Plato's reforming side as leading to his rationalistic insistence on system[16] and ignoring the interdependence of system and internal conviction: a rational objectivism that denies subjective individualism. However, within Plato's argument insisting on the unity of the city, Oakeshott sees a truth many modern thinkers have ignored. Plato, and Aristotle, understand human beings to be the most they can be *within* a state. The *polis* exists, Aristotle says in the *Politics*, not for living but for living well (1252b29). The thought here, as Oakeshott understands it, is that human beings are nothing without the state, that, quoting Nettleship, "There is no such thing as an individual in the abstract, a human being literally independent of all others" (*Rep I*:63; 1897, 177), and quoting Bradley, "The State without the individual is no more an abstraction than the individual without the State" (*Rep I*:63v).

This view is reinforced in a number of places in Oakeshott's reading of the *Republic*. Thrasymachus' argument that "Injustice, when it comes into being on a sufficient scale, is mightier, freer, and more masterful than justice" (344c) is followed in

---

association and a powerful augment to the view of the state as an enterprise association (*OHC* 273).

[15] This view is further reinforced, following Lutoslawski (1897) and Stewart (1909) (both of whom Oakeshott was acquainted with), in grouping the 'Socratic' dialogues as the 'earliest', followed by the later more Platonic groupings as the systemization increases.

[16] As we saw in the previous chapter, in a later essay Oakeshott gives Plato the title of the "father of demonstrative political discourse" (*RIP* 82).

Oakeshott's notebook with a reference to T.H. Green's lecture on political obligation. In this lecture, Green is taking issue with the social contract theorists (Spinoza, Hobbes, Locke, and even Rousseau) in the separation they presume between individuals on the one hand and the state on the other.[17] Green's argument is that individuals (the rights they have and the freedoms they enjoy) are inseparable from the community they are in, that the community finds its unity in a shared understanding of what is good, and that the formal governing apparatus of the state is an attempt to give fuller reality to that conception of the good" (1886, 428, 430-31, 444).

Oakeshott's critique of Glaucon's social contract is that, though it captures some truth about the community being a tacit contract and that "society must have force to back it up", nevertheless, referencing Green again, it is will (not force) that is the basis of the state (*Rep I*:26v-26). Or, again in Adeimantus' objection that these people are hardly made happy and Socrates' reply that happiness is a harmony—like the beauty of a statue it is not an abstraction but a relation (*Rep I*:50)—we see the embedded social nature of the individual.[18]

Nevertheless, as we have seen, Oakeshott is following Hegel in his criticism of Plato's failure to recognize the significance, however dependent on society, of the individual. However, Oakeshott has an implicit critique of Hegel as not being concrete and historical enough in his treatment of Plato. If we return to Oakeshott's third essay in *On Human Conduct*, the idea of individuality Hegel is concerned with may not have been available to Plato. As Oakeshott traces the development of the modern state, the modern individual appears on the

---

[17] It is not surprising that the line of argument is very closely followed by Bosanquet in his *Philosophical Theory of the State* (1923), which Oakeshott references a number of times in the notebooks. Bosanquet singles out in addition to the usual social contract theorists, Mill, Spencer, and Kant as positing the atomistic individual *versus* the state.

[18] Just how social and just how individual Oakeshott imagines human beings to be has been a source of considerable debate in the Oakeshott literature. The debate has centered around how Hobbesian (liberal individualism) versus how Hegelian (culturally and historically embedded) Oakeshott views the individual. See Franco (1990), especially chapter 5, for a more Hegelian reading of Oakeshott, and Gerencser (2000) for a very skeptical Hobbesian account. For an account of the individual as more culturally and morally situated see Coats (2000), especially chapter 3. Oakeshott's reading of Plato may shed some light on this debate by revealing the nature of Oakeshott's early idealism.

scene in sufficient numbers when the recognition that human beings are reflective intelligences comes to be viewed as "the emblem of human dignity and as a condition for each individual to explore, to cultivate, to make the most of, and to enjoy as an opportunity rather than suffer as a burden" (1975, 236). This can only happen when an increasing number of activities are not directed by the political regime, are not put in the service of the regime, but left to individuals to decide upon. Only then can the practice of deliberating and choosing develop into a disposition

> to recognize imagining, deliberating, wanting, choosing, and acting not as costs incurred in seeking enjoyments but as themselves enjoyments, the exercise of a gratifying self-determination or personal autonomy (*OHC* 236).

It would be hard to imagine the individualism Hegel describes as available, in practice, in the Greek world and thus available as something to theorize. The *polis* remained the central locus of one's identity both in the imaginings of someone like Pericles, where the glory, victory, and autonomy of the city is what is most significant,[19] in the Platonic city in speech where each contributes to the justice and good of the city by tending to their own business, or in Aristotle's insistence that one is more fully actualizing one's human potential when exercising *phronesis* over that which is more complete and self-sufficient (i.e., the *polis* or public thing).

Though Plato may rightly be criticized for his lack of appreciation of the subjective freedom involved in one's obligations to the city, it could hardly be the fault of Plato that he is unable to theorize an individuality barely intimated in the Greek experience (except perhaps in a nascent form in Socrates). It would be difficult, if not impossible, to put it slightly differently, for Plato to theorize something other than a teleocracy. To imagine, with Hegel, that the unity of human society can only be obtained *through* individualized diversity and the greater "the differentiation the greater the unity", would be to expect too much of Plato given the Greek *sittlichkeit* (*Rep I*:30v). If the state is a reflection of the disposition of the individuals who make up the state and these individuals are not disposed to individualism let alone to celebrate it as the emblem of their humanity, it is easy to see why Plato would not have theorized

---

[19] See Pericles' 'Funeral Oration' in Thucydides (1982, II:35–46).

the state in these terms: the necessary conditions would not have been available for him to do so.

Plato and the Modern European State

This brings us back to the modern European state as Oakeshott theorizes it and to a final Platonic theme in Oakeshott's thinking and a final critique of Plato. If one of the things Oakeshott shared with Plato was a belief that the state is a reflection of the disposition of those who make-up the state, the tension in Plato's disposition has an analogy in the tension of dispositions Oakeshott sees reflected in the modern European state.

As Oakeshott puts it in the third essay of *On Human Conduct*, the office of government, in a modern European state, also has a dual character objectified in the administrative history of the state. This dual character, in turn, is reflected in and is a reflection of the dispositions of the associates that make up the state. The state, Oakeshott says, is best viewed as "an unresolved tension between two irreconcilable dispositions" (*OHC* 201). One disposition makes possible the analogy of the state to that of a *universitas*. Here the state is viewed as "persons associated in respect of some identified common purpose, in pursuit of some acknowledged substantive end, or in the promotion of some specified enduring interest" (*OHC* 203). But, the other disposition makes the analogy of the state as a *societas* more appropriate. In this view, the relationship of associates in a state is understood "not as an engagement in an enterprise to pursue some common substantive purpose or to promote a common interest" but that of "loyalty to one another" denoted by the "kindred word 'legality'". The relationship is "a formal relationship in terms of rules", a "pact or agreement . . . to acknowledge the authority of certain conditions of acting" but not determining the substantive choices of what actions to perform (*OHC* 201). It is these two dispositions in human beings that give rise to these two visions of the state: the desire on the one hand to be independent and self-regulating individuals suggests a relationship of being bound together only by law; the desire to live in a state united by a view of substantive justice on the other hand suggests a relationship of a shared end or purpose.

Oakeshott clearly saw the modern European state as characterized by this tension or, put another way, by systematic ambiguity over whether the state should be a formal organization or a substantive one. There are clearly early echoes here in Plato of this vision. Whether Plato, absent a more fully developed view of the individual, saw clearly the tension between these two alternative ideas of the state is not clear.[20] Oakeshott's reading of Socrates, as we have seen in Chapter 3, comes very close to formulating an idea of an association primarily in terms of a rule of law. Much later in an intriguing set of footnotes in *On Human Conduct*, Oakeshott suggests Aristotle came close to advancing such a view and that his distinction between constitution or office of government and the aims or ends of government is a necessary prelude to thinking of government as not about achieving a substantive vision of the common good.[21]

One disposition Plato has, as we have seen, is that of a reformer. Out of this disposition comes Plato's desire for system, a vision of the ultimate *telos* upon which society might finally be rationally organized. This vision would be and has been appealing to a modern individual (or, rather, individual *manqué*), recently deprived of the comfort of a defined identity and thrown back upon himself to construct his own. If the Good could finally be settled, this disposition might turn into the intolerance of difference characterized by Oakeshott's anti-individual (*OHC* 278).

Plato's other disposition, however is a philosophic one. This side of Plato has its roots in the "sceptical, enquiring spirit" of Socrates and is an irreconcilable counterpoint to Plato's reforming impulse.[22] While keeping in mind Oakeshott's pub-

---

[20] Timothy Fuller suggested to me Plato may have been aware of the dialectical tension between a view of the state where a substantive good was the aim and the view of the state as a formal, legal association. Whether Oakeshott saw Plato as advancing the view of a dialectical tension here is difficult to definitively defend from the notebooks on Plato, Oakeshott's Cambridge Lectures, and Oakeshott's published work, though it may be he held this view.

[21] I am grateful to Noël O'Sullivan for drawing my attention to the fact that something like an ancient view of the state as a formal organization is intimated in Aristotle and Plato that Oakeshott may have identified and been attracted to (See *OHC* 167n.1, 192n.1).

[22] It is interesting to note here that Oakeshott thought Socrates to combine, without necessarily being able to resolve, a social conservatism with a philosophical radicalism. "Socrates was a conservative in that he equated the just and the legal. A real loyalty and love of law" (*EGP* 12). He also "taught men to think and to question everything. He refused to cease his teaching in spite of prohibition. All except conscience must be under the control of the State" (*EGP* 12).

lished argument in *On Human Conduct* that Plato erred in thinking the philosopher had anything useful to say to those in the cave and that they were perfectly capable of getting on in the cave without the philosopher, Oakeshott is much less severe on Plato in the notebooks. Early on, and without question, Oakeshott thought Plato made an error in insisting the philosopher be of direct service to the political realm (*Rep I*:78, 79, 72v). Yet, Oakeshott sees Plato's philosophical impulse as strong. He has a profound "sense of the immensity of knowledge" akin to that of "Pascal's scepticism" (*Rep I*:78). In his treatment of Plato's discussion of the Good, Oakeshott remarks that "All through the *Republic* you feel the true humbleness of Socrates. We do not know all things. Life is very great, and not easily to be understood" (*Rep I*:74). This naturally pulls in the opposite direction.

Oakeshott's understanding of Plato's argument on the sovereignty of philosophy reflects the dual disposition of Plato. The philosopher must be in the service of the state. However, Oakeshott interprets this service the philosopher may give to the state as much broader than that involved in actually ruling or directly influencing the rule in a particular regime. "The relation between society and great men should be one of mutual recognition and service" (*Rep I*:79). We must recall, Oakeshott notes in this series of notes, "We are not God's [*sic*], nor children, but men among men" (*Rep I*:79).[23] Next to this quote Oakeshott references the *Laws* (739b). The suggestion seems to be that given the limitations of human beings, a second best city is what is required as a practical alternative.[24] Nevertheless, "The great man must remember that he owes a tremendous amount of his greatness and character to society;

---

[23]   Bosanquet, in his *Companion*, has an illuminating reading of Socrates' answer to the question of the practicability of the city in speech and philosophers becoming kings. Plato does not avoid the question, but "in perfect logical order, when he turns to the question of possibility begins by explaining that between this abstraction and its realization in historical fact there is undoubtedly a condition interposed; he then proceeds to state this condition (viz., a scientific treatment of politics), and subsequently to show, from the connection both of the ideal and of its condition with the central realities of life and mind, that the degree in which the condition is fulfilled will also be the degree in which the essentials of his 'illustration' will become historic fact" (1906, 200–201).

[24]   This is the reading Nettleship gives to this section of the *Republic*. In the *Laws* Plato "proceeds to show what he thinks the nearest practicable approximation to the institutions" of the *Republic* are (1897, 185n1).

and he will willingly serve society in return" (*Rep I*:79v). But, what is this service? Is it for philosophers to be kings? Oakeshott does not focus on this 'service' being directly political in nature and one might usefully compare his essay "The Claims of Politics" where one's service may be to *abstain from* engaging in politics (*RPML* 94). The similarity to Socrates' argument that his private way of life has been a gift to the city is unmistakable.

This disposition in Plato—the more detached, humble, philosophically inquisitive side—has a strong parallel in the disposition of the *socius* in a modern civil association. It is the skeptical disposition to imagine, not that the Good does not exist, but that it may be exceedingly difficult if not impossible to fully know the Good let alone use it as a guide for political arrangements. Absent a clear roadmap for human beings, bereft of a comprehensive agreement about our ends to which we might all direct our energies, life might alternatively be viewed as an adventure, and our relationship to others as a *civitas peregrina*: an association, not of pilgrims travelling to a common destination, but of adventurers each responding as best he can to the ordeal of consciousness in a world composed of others of his kind, each the inheritor of the imaginative achievements (moral and intellectual) of those who have gone before and joined in a variety of prudential practices, but here partners in a practice of civility the rules of which are not devices for satisfying substantive wants and whose obligations create no symbiotic relationship (*OHC* 243).

To modern individuals with a strong historical sensibility and a Socratic humility about the limits and possibilities of human beings, both in action and in thought, the state as a *societas* would be more appealing. It establishes an authority to lay down rules of civility while maintaining a sphere for individual self-expression and activity. To a modern individual drawn to the comfort of a comprehensive roadmap that provides relief from the burden of making often very difficult choices, the state as a *universitas* may be more appropriate. "It may be true", Oakeshott suggests, "that, hidden in human character, there are two powerful and contrary dispositions, neither strong enough to defeat or to put to fight the other" (*OHC* 323). These two dispositions find an early expression in Plato and account for the ambivalent character of the activities of the modern European state.

Chapter VI

The Study of Politics

New Sophists and New Platonists

"The *Leviathan*", Oakeshott claims in his introduction to his 1946 edition of Hobbes's work

> is the greatest, perhaps the sole, masterpiece of political philosophy written in the English language. And the history of our civilization can provide only a few works of similar scope and achievement to set beside it (*RIP* 223).

Oakeshott makes a similar claim in this introduction about Plato's *Republic* and Hegel's *Philosophy of Right*. This is extraordinary praise for these books. Is it exaggerated? Upon what grounds does Oakeshott hope to convince us of this rather extravagant claim? His defense rests on a particular understanding of how one should approach the history of political thought.

A persistent thread in the previous chapters has been that the early Greeks (the pre-Socratics, Socrates, and Plato) play a key role in helping Oakeshott articulate a view of how to study a book like Hobbes's *Leviathan* or Plato's *Republic*: it is a view that continues to be useful in helping us navigate differing conceptions of what is to be found in the study of the history of political thought. Plato himself has been shown to be both help and hindrance in this pursuit. That is, Plato conflates two viewpoints that, Oakeshott insists, with Socrates, are best maintained as separate: the viewpoint of the reformer and the viewpoint of the philosopher.

A careful analysis of some important distinctions Oakeshott makes about political thought and a critical look at what might, with some risk, be called Oakeshott's methodology, reveals a more satisfactory conception of the possibilities of political philosophy than that offered by Plato and others.[1] It helps avoid the dead ends often provoked by recent arguments over canons, texts, contexts, and timeless questions. It shows the complementary nature of historical and philosophical approaches to politics while pointing out the limitations the former approach to the history of political thought as conceived by Quentin Skinner.[2]

What I investigate first in this chapter is how Oakeshott saw the reforming side of Plato leading to a particular justification for the study of politics. It is a view that underpins an approach to political philosophy that continues to have wide appeal and influence today. Then, I lay out Oakeshott's alternative — an alternative Oakeshott develops with the help of the Socratic/philosophic side of Plato. Finally I address the contemporary approach of Skinner to show the limited perspective of this approach for understanding the history of political thought.

Plato's Reform Politics

As we have seen Oakeshott understands Plato to be moved by two distinct impulses — that of the philosopher and that of the reformer. It was the practical desire to reform that distracted Plato, ultimately compromising the quality of his philosophizing. Together with the picture of the general development of philosophy articulated in Oakeshott's Cambridge lecturers as the slow refinement of the practice of philosophy, Oakeshott clearly understood Plato to insist on a definite and narrow reason for the study of politics and a particular character for the education involved. Not surprisingly, the reforming side of Plato urges the study for practical reasons. We saw in the previous chapter that Plato understood the state to be a reflection

---

[1]   I am using 'methodology' in the broadest sense to mean an orderly approach or practice to the study of politics. I in no way want to suggest that Oakeshott is advocating the position, indefensible in light of his argument in "Rationalism in Politics" and "Rational Conduct" (*RIP* 5ff., 99ff.), that in order to do good political philosophy one must be armed with a surefire set of independently premeditated, abstract principles to get started philosophizing. Rather, it is to recognize that the principles spring from the concrete activity of philosophizing itself. As Minogue has said, and this is clearly reflected in Oakeshott's writings, "Oakeshott's inclination was to reject methodological formulae and to rely upon a philosophical self-consciousness about the precise relevance of the questions being asked and answered" (Minogue 1993, viii).

[2]   See for example Saxonhouse (1993) for a survey of some of the debates.

of the disposition of those who compose the state. Education becomes important, for how those come to have the dispositions they do influences the character of the state. "Education and public opinion are, in the end, the upholders of the state — not legislation", Oakeshott sees Plato as saying (Rep I:50). There must be a 'spiritual marriage' between internal (the soul) and external conditions, but if education is well executed early in life all of the rest will follow. A good education and a good state follow and reinforce one another in a "wave like" action and reaction, which is an "idea of natural tendency to progress" that is "rare in Plato" (*Rep I*:51).

While Oakeshott does not disagree with the diagnosis that the state is a reflection of the individuals who compose the state, as seen in the previous chapter, he is critical of the remedy Plato proposes. Plato (recall from the *Republic*) opts for a monastic response of removing 'bad' influences to educate and harmonize the soul. But Plato also argues that a sufficient knowledge of the Good will have the effect on the soul of harmonizing one's internal conditions and thus the external conditions. When Socrates is pressed about the practicability of the city, he responds by laying out the conditions necessary for the city to come into being. The reason a people's thoughts or ideals (on justice, on the ideal city) are not actualized is because there is an insufficient grasp of the ideal itself. If the Good itself were fully grasped and those who had full knowledge of the Good also were in a position of power, the just regime could come into being for Plato. From this point, one could either say that the Good is knowable in some clear and definitive way or one could say that philosophy is the attempt to know the Good while recognizing the difficulty of every attaining this complete knowledge. Plato the reformer would be optimistic about the possibility of knowing the Good, for to know the Good would actually put one in the position of being able to construct the demonstratively correct regime. The more skeptical, Socratic, and philosophic Plato would not abandon the search for the Good but would be skeptical of ever attaining the good itself and hence would place more significance on the search than on the outcome of the search.

The initial issue remains. Plato did not separate practical, moral questions from philosophical questions. At the bottom of knowledge is the Good for the reforming Plato, whereas the more Socratic side of Plato is the skeptical inquiring spirit of philosophy that leaves open the question of getting to the bottom of knowledge. The dialectic procedure Socrates uses to study politics and the state, as well as justice and virtue, is "*critical* and its result *categorical*", but not moral for Oakeshott (*Rep I*:83). Oakeshott is following Bosanquet in most of this reading, but conspicuously leaves out the moral part of Bosanquet's commentary. Specifically Oakeshott does not record Bosanquet's reading that "Dialectic is, to conclude, the apprehension of *moral* and *religious* truth: of the good" (1906, 302).

There are a number of different versions of this Platonic understanding of the relationship between goodness and truth. Bosanquet, in Oakeshott's own time, clearly saw the study of the history of philosophy as ultimately uncovering a moral truth that could help guide society. Alasdair MacIntyre in his continuing quest to revive and renew ancient moral thinking has recently argued for the reintroduction of moral and theological questions into the university. The university ought to be "an arena of conflict in which the most fundamental type of moral and theological disagreement was accorded recognition" (1990, 231). In a current volume of *Political Theory* devoted to the question of what political theory is, Ruth Grant argued for bringing together what she sees as a humanist approach to the study of politics and a scientific approach. What is interesting is the unmistakably Platonic understanding of political theory she advances.

> At bottom, political theory is an extension of a natural, daily activity. In this it resembles ethics. Every human being engages in some form of ethical reflection as a condition of action. Ethics as an academic discipline is an extension of, not a departure from that daily activity (2002, 588).

The analogy is that political theory is a mere extension of practical political thinking, only more "critical, constructive, historical and sensitive to contingency, skeptical, and conserving" (2002, 591). But, and aside from nods in a different direction,[3] if this is so then the political theorist is in a better position to make political judgments, being the one who studies judgment. Is this not a reiteration of the Platonic position

---

[3]   Grant references Oakeshott's distinction between practical (traditional) knowledge and technical knowledge at 587.

that knowledge is virtue, and by extension, knowledge of the 'Good' could create a perfect harmonious political order?

Each of these beliefs and positions, if taken to its logical conclusion, results in a similar view of the study of politics than would at first appear. The view that the dividing line is between a timeless questions approach to political theory and a radically historicized approach to political theory turns out to be much more difficult to maintain. The study of and reflection on politics is viewed as essentially about the same thing: trying to answer practical political-ethical questions that a society or societies might face or be facing. In fact, most reflection is viewed in this manner, whether in science, history, philosophy, or practical life the conclusion these views all seem to point to is that reflection is primarily about solving practical problems (whether timeless or not). These different ways of thinking, however, may be more or less mutually exclusive, as Oakeshott maintains: not every political thinker today, let alone across the history of political thought, is asking the same questions about politics. Oakeshott helps us appreciate the different kinds of reflection (especially the different kinds of reflection on politics).

Oakeshott's Study of Politics

Oakeshott's approach to the history of political thought has the advantage of distinguishing different kinds or levels of political reflection and of allowing us to see that some contexts are more appropriate than others for understanding a particular political text. What he is most interested in is the philosophical context and it is in this context he maintains where the quality of a philosophic work must be judged.

Oakeshott was acutely aware of the importance of context for understanding any work of political thinking. "All explanation, all interpretation", Oakeshott says in an often overlooked essay written in 1938,

> may be seen as a matter of deciding upon and examining the appropriate setting for what is to be explained and of exhibiting it in its place in that setting. Given a 'text', something partially disconnected, obscure, imperfectly conceived, explanation is the attempt to find the 'context' and to relate text and context so that they become a single whole (*CJP* 350).

Oakeshott, as we shall see, distinguishes many different kinds of reflections on politics and the related utterances (or texts) that emerge from these different reflections. The explanation or meaning of these are revealed by relating the utterance to the appropriate context.

Oakeshott insists that the context in which we must judge a work of political philosophy is historically rather extensive. "[T]he context of the masterpiece itself", Oakeshott maintains, "the setting in which its meaning is revealed, can in the nature of things be nothing narrower than the history of political philosophy" (*RIP* 223). This, at first glance, does not get us very far, for the history of political philosophy is itself vague, abstract, and contestable. Unless we are prepared for what to expect out of the history of political philosophy, we have made little progress. Indeed, it is a central contention of this chapter, and of the larger study, that what we expect from the history of political thought, presupposes, perhaps constitutes, a methodology. As Oakeshott says in *Experience and Its Modes*, "[t]he method is correlative to the matter; when we consider the one we are considering the other also" (*EM* 95).[4] One of the critical insights Oakeshott has to offer is that the context within which one considers a text presupposes the type of enquiry or set of reflections the text is occupied with. With that in mind, what we seek is the appropriate context(s) within which to understand a text in the history of political thought.

In his course of lectures entitled "A Study of Political Thought" given at the London School of Economics in the 1950s and 1960s, Oakeshott tells us a bit about how he understands the history of political thought. There he makes clear he is going to present an historical study: a study that attempts to explain political beliefs by situating them in their historical context. That is, the study of the history of political thought begins from the point of view in which "nothing which men have thought or done is intelligible except in its own context or circumstances" (*LSE* 32). And, he says what he has to present will be neither a continuous history of political thought or a cumulative one. Neither will his lectures contain a complete history (of the Plato to NATO variety) nor necessarily a progressive history. Oakeshott was well aware of the complexity of the history of political thought and recognized that a com-

---

[4]   See also pp. 175, 210.

plete history, if not impossible, among other implications, would suggest all reflections on politics are of the same sort. Instead he recognizes qualitatively different types of reflections on politics. Philosophical reflections are one sort that have "gone on in every society which is politically conscious and intellectually alive" (*RIP* 65). There might be continuities among the practitioners of this radically critical activity of philosophy, but the continuities do not cut across the whole set of reflections on politics we have from the past. Nor do the philosophical reflections we have from the past reflect an evolutionary pattern of advance. One might usefully contrast Oakeshott here with Burke. Oakeshott, erroneously, is often said to have strong affinities with Burke in his understanding of the value of tradition. Burke values the past as "the pride of the human intellect, which with all its defects, redundancies and errors is the collected reason of ages" ([1790] 1955, 108). Alternatively, Oakeshott says, "I cannot detect a history of political thought which reveals a gradual accumulation of political wisdom and understanding. Indeed, I cannot detect anything which could properly correspond to the expression '*the* history of political thought'" (*LSE* 32). In rather modest language, he explains, "[w]hat I think I can see is different peoples, at different times, in different intellectual and physical circumstances, engaging in politics in different ways and finding different things to think about it. And sometimes I think I can see some sort of an explanation for these different peoples having had the thoughts which they did have. And that is about all" (*LSE* 33).

Oakeshott goes on, however, to argue that political thought or reflection is of different kinds or takes place at different levels. Oakeshott identifies, in a number of places, these various kinds or levels of political thought and makes a rather sharp distinction between prescriptive and descriptive utterances (*MPME* 13-15; *RIP* 223-25). The significance of these levels and types of reflection on politics is that they are concerned with different kinds of questions about political experience (*MPME* 13). His major distinction is between thought and reflection on politics in the service of political action and thought and reflection that is an attempt at explanation. This is, of course, the central concern Oakeshott has had with Plato: he is a philosopher *and* a reformer and is unable to keep these two separate.

Levels and Varieties of Political Reflection

Practical Reflection

The first level of reflection on politics Oakeshott identifies is what might be called practical reflection on politics.

> [I]n the end, the only means we have of coming to understand any political experience, our own or that of another time and people, is by listening to the political utterance and by getting to know its political words and how they are used (*LSE* 41).

Oakeshott begins his LSE lectures in this manner with an examination of the immediate political context that surrounds a political text (*LSE* 42). This is how we all began in our understanding of politics, with what has (unfortunately) been called political socialization. We learn about politics by having particular experiences that are identified as political, and we express our understanding of those experiences in words and actions – in the vocabulary we use and in our performances.

Oakeshott begins his study of political thought in his LSE lectures with a close look at the vocabulary of politics used in a particular time and justifies this approach.

> It is these words which express political beliefs. It is these words, and the way in which they are used in political argument or in the expression of political opinions, which tell us how a people thinks when it thinks about politics (*LSE* 40).

In order to understand for example what Pericles meant in saying "We have a form of government that does not emulate our neighbors ... in name it is called a democracy on account of it being administered in the interest not of the few but the many" (Thucydides 1998, II:37), we must understand the context in which they were uttered, both the time and place but also the set of beliefs this people (the Athenians) had about democracy, government, war, honor, justice or citizenship. "What we are seeking", Oakeshott says, "is to understand political utterances in their place in what may be called the political culture of a people" (*LSE* 42). This is an historical study of language as it reveals the thinking of a people, and Oakeshott notes it is a "history of men thinking, not a 'history' of abstract disembodied 'ideas'" (*LSE* 42). This is no doubt where we begin in our understanding of politics, our own politics or another's. We begin with the language of politics as it is used in politics and seek to understand how this political language is used, and what it reveals about the thinking of those who use it. This is the unmistakable approach Socrates takes in the first book of the *Republic*.

Even a cursory survey of political utterances immediately reveals a number of different types, or different levels, of political reflection on politics, and that the most frequently encountered is a type of reflection that uses the currently available vocabulary of politics to engage in politics itself.

When President Bush in his 2002 State of the Union Address said,

> America will lead by defending liberty and justice because they are right and true and unchanging for all people everywhere. No nation owns these aspirations and no nation is exempt from them. We have no intention of imposing our culture, but America will always stand firm for the non-negotiable demands of human dignity, the rule of law, limits on the power of the state, respect for women, private property, free speech, equal justice and religious tolerance[5]

we have no problem understanding what he means. We recognize the words he uses and how he uses them. We are able to identify what he says as a political utterance designed to evoke courage and unity; to persuade and justify; to diagnose and to recommend. In short, it is meant to have a practical impact and it has this logical design.[6] It reflects, as Oakeshott says, "thought in the service of political action" (*MPME* 13). It is thinking and talking about politics "whose design is to diagnose political situations, to recommend responses to be made to them, to choose and to decide what shall be done or to defend or justify in argument what has been done" (*LSE* 42). It may involve descriptive statements but the force of the statements is prescriptive. What makes it practical is its prescriptive character.

We might respond with practical reflections ourselves: 'He is right in his diagnosis'; 'His budget plan is unlikely to achieve the stated goals'; 'More people should do community service'. The meaning of Bush's words, and indeed what is

---

[5] Bush 2002, A22.
[6] The logical design of practical political utterances is revealed in the prescriptive character. "For all political deliberation, all deliberation about what to or what not to do, entails beliefs about what is better or worse. All argument designed to recommend an action is designed to show, not only that *these* will be its consequences, but also that they are to be preferred to any other" (*RIP* 91).

probably Bush's intent or the illocutionary force of his words, are gathered from the immediate context of time and place: post-September 11, the State of the Union Address, etc., and from the logical design of his utterances.

There might be explanatory responses to Bush's speech (e.g., the 'political commentary' both before and after such events). The form of this explanation (which at times is very difficult to separate from prescription) is to broaden or narrow the political context: 'it is strategic in light of the legislative context and the possibility of getting more of his budget priorities through the Congress'; 'it reflects a political maturity and vision lacking in previous utterances'; 'it shows the effective use of the "bully" pulpit', etc.

General Principles

Reflection, however, might take a rather different turn in approaching Bush's speech. The concern might not be to weigh the argument in order to consider whether one agrees or disagrees either at the concrete level or an ideological level with his proposals. Rather, one might attempt to explain the speech itself in terms of some more general ideas: 'his speech reflects liberalism's basic tenets'; 'it embodies the belief in American exceptionalism'; or 'it reveals a particularly American response to international relations'. The aim here is to understand more fully some political experience by attempting to describe or explain it in terms of the broader political culture of a people or, as Oakeshott puts it, to "abridge our political experience into a doctrine [liberalism], which may be used, as a scientist uses hypothesis, to explore its intimations" (*RIP* 65).

Or, take a different example, one drawn from a pedagogical approach used to teach American politics. In the study of the American political system there has been a continuing debate over whether this system is best described as a majoritarian, a pluralist, or an elite system. Each of these 'models' are attempts not necessarily at prescribing what type of political system we ought to have, that is, practical reflections on politics, but are explanatory or descriptive reflections on politics (though, of course, they have been used in both capacities). They are attempts to make sense of American politics by abridging the whole complex goings-on into a set of general descriptive principles and in so doing, as Oakeshott says, they

may help us understand our own politics in the way "a carica-
ture reveals the potentialities of a face" (*RIP* 58). Now these
reflections are of a qualitatively different sort. They are uttered
in the indicative mood rather than the imperative mood; they
are reflections moving in the direction of explanation and
understanding rather than reflections in the pursuit of some
action.

Philosophical Level

But there is another (though this doesn't round out an exhaus-
tive list), much rarer, level of political thinking Oakeshott
identifies as philosophical reflection. "It appears", he says

> when what is being attempted is neither to determine upon policy
> nor to make sense of political desires and actions by understand-
> ing them in the idiom of general principles, but to consider the
> place of government and political activity on the map of human
> activity in general. The questions being asked at this level of
> thought are: What are we really doing when we are engaged in
> political activity? What really is this activity called 'governing'?
> (*MPME* 14).

Philosophy is concerned to consider this activity, politics, "on
the map of human activity in general" (*MPME* 15), or "on the
map of our total experience"(*RIP* 65).[7]

It is not hard to see that the context has thus been enlarged
quite significantly while the explanatory urge remains in place
at this level of reflection. This expansion of context signals a
new order of enquiry: the questions are no longer How do we
understand this particular instance of political action?, or How
do we best characterize the concrete way a people has prac-
ticed its politics?, but How do we understand politics in relationship to everything else that is going on around us? It is this
context, asking these questions, that makes it a philosophical
investigation. But, further, what makes it philosophical is the
attempt to explain and not to prescribe; to attempt to understand as fully as possible and not to express desire and
aversion or approval and disapproval.

Oakeshott identifies then a number of levels of reflection on
politics, he has made a distinction between prescriptive and
descriptive utterances about politics, and has insisted that the

---

[7]   See also *LSE* 101, where Aristotle's reflections in his *Politics* are said to be
philosophical on account of "establishing the place of politics on a kind of
intellectual map of the cosmos".

meaning of a political text or utterance is revealed by locating the utterance in its appropriate context. One of the difficulties to be noticed, and Oakeshott recognizes this, is that in practice these different levels are not easily distinguished in a given set of reflections on politics (in a text). A speaker or writer might easily move from one level of reflection to another. Hobbes, for example, slides easily from immediate concerns with the English Civil War to identifying complex human activities in terms of general concepts to articulating the concept of authority. Politics is one of the most difficult subjects of study because of the mixture of these qualitatively different types of statements, and because the vocabulary of politics continually invites the understanding of politics in its own language (i.e., in solely prescriptive terms). In Oakeshott's essay on "The Study of 'Politics' in a University", he notes the difficulty this poses.

> Politics offers the most difficult of all 'literatures,' the most difficult collection of 'texts,' in connection with which to learn to handle and manage the languages of explanation: the idiom of the material to be studied is ever ready to impose itself upon the manner in which it is studied (*RIP* 217-18).

Despite this difficulty (a difficulty perhaps never ultimately overcome) one of the major consequences of distinguishing these different levels of political reflection is that they help us identify the meaning of someone's words. Some contexts are more appropriate than others for determining their meaning.[8] Bush's state of the union address is best understood, not as a philosophical investigation, nor as an attempt to explain events in terms of general principles, nor as a wholly descriptive statement, but as a set of practical reflections with pre-

---

[8]   The failure to articulate the appropriate context to reveal the meaning of some human utterance was a continuing issue for Oakeshott. One of the greatest philosophical errors one can make for Oakeshott is to make a category mistake and thus to render what one has to say irrelevant. In his first course of lectures at Cambridge, he takes great pains to point out different definitions of the state (legal, historical, etc.) in order to point toward what a philosophical definition of the state is like. One way to characterize the error Oakeshott saw Plato making (perhaps unavoidably in his time) is to say that he failed to keep clear qualitatively different categories of logical utterance: philosophical definition is as irrelevant to practical politics as knowing water is made up of hydrogen and oxygen is to a seaside painter. A persistent theme in *Experience and Its Modes* (1933) is to highlight the mistake of thinking one mode of explanation can inform another, that a scientific explanation, for example, can inform an historic one.

scriptive force. All meaning is not had in one particular context, but neither is it the case that a set of reflections on politics has their most cogent meaning in just the context of practical politics. One of Oakeshott's continuing aims is to try to avoid irrelevance by attempting to understand something in an inappropriate context. To mistake Bush's utterances on justice as qualitatively the same as Plato's utterances on justice is to condemn one or the other, or both, to irrelevance.

The Philosophical Context

What Oakeshott means by philosophical reflections on politics then should be clear. He is not talking about reflections on politics with an aim to effect immediate political action, nor is he referring to reflections on politics that explain a set of utterances by distilling a set of general principles said to reflect the political culture in which they were uttered. What he is talking about is philosophical reflections on politics, which is a level of political reflection that attempts to place politics on the map of human activity in general or on the map of our total experience. It involves asking the questions: What is political activity? How does it relate to other activities that constitute the totality of our experience?

Oakeshott has defined philosophy, in *Experience and Its Modes* as "experience without presupposition, reservation, arrest or modification" (1933, 2). Or again, in *On Human Conduct*, he says

> theorizing has revealed itself as an unconditional adventure in which every achievement of understanding is an invitation to investigate itself and where the reports a theorist makes to himself are interim triumphs of temerity over scruple (1975, 11).

What could Oakeshott possibly mean by this? In order to understand what Oakeshott has in mind it is useful to pursue how the levels mentioned earlier lead to this understanding of a philosophical reflection on politics and to return to the ideas of text and context in this connection.

Bush's speech makes the most sense, is the most coherent, as reflection in the service of politics, and the immediate context of its being delivered provides a more complete explanation or description of its meaning than others. It is hard to imagine, let alone provide evidence for, the speech as an effort to think philosophically about politics. To understand his speech as a coherent philosophical set of reflections on politics is to place the text in an inappropriate context. The context where it makes most sense is the context of American culture at a particular time and place.

How does one best understand a text like Robert Dahl's *Who Governs*? Presumably it would be a mistake to find the meaning of this text in the immediate context of the politics of New Haven and it hardly could be described as an attempt to change the particular policies of New Haven. What makes the most sense is to place it in the context of explanatory works of a particular kind. It is an attempt to explain the political world before him, New Haven (and perhaps to be able to extrapolate to the larger political system), by articulating a set of general principles (Pluralism).

How does one understand a text like *Leviathan*? Is it equivalent to Bush's speech or Dahl's book? Recall, Oakeshott said of Hobbes's *Leviathan* that the appropriate context to understand this work is the history of political thought. What this means in part is that this work should not be seen primarily as a particular intervention into seventeenth century British politics, nor as an attempt to describe those politics by distilling a descriptive set of general principles. What context is the appropriate one to understand a philosophical work in the history of political thought that gives it its meaning?

> [W]here the purpose of reflection is to determine meaning; because the meaning is not something which belongs to the text or the context, neither of which is fixed independently of the other, but is properly assumed to be in the unity which text and context together compose, and in which, as text and context, they cease to exist (*EM* 151).

In finding the one, we will find the other. What is necessary to unite the two is not just an acquaintance with the text, but also an understanding of the context, which in the case of a philosophical work is the history of philosophical reflections. What is the nature of this history?

The Philosophical Context as a Practice/Tradition

As we have seen, to be philosophical about anything for Oakeshott is to seek coherence; to try to make sense of incongruous elements in our experience. This is a characteristic of all reflection. What makes it philosophical is the impulse of the philosopher to not limit the context within which he or she thinks about something like politics. Bush's reflections on politics are understandable and indeed limited to the immediate political context; Dahl's book is most coherently seen in the context of attempts to make sense of American politics. Plato's *Republic* may have characteristics of both of these, but it also (and perhaps more so than these others) is characterized by the attempt to understand politics in the context of everything else that he experienced and understood. It is an attempt to describe or explain politics and its relationship to other activities that make up a human life as fully and completely as possible. In doing so, as a philosopher, he is fully submitting to a 'mood' present in all reflection.[9]

Oakeshott identifies this mood throughout his works as a profoundly skeptical one. Philosophical enquiry is peculiar because it is governed by a radical skepticism with regard to every stopping place that is suggested. This was the skepticism we saw Oakeshott notice and appreciate in Socrates and admire in the Socratic side of Plato. In a very early essay on the topic Oakeshott says it is a skepticism that "is suspicious of every attempt to limit the enquiry" (*CJP* 348). Again in *Experience and Its Modes* it is characterized as "experience without presupposition, reservation, arrest or modification" (1933, 2). It is the disposition to view every "platform of conditional understanding [as] something of a prison from which he seeks release", as Oakeshott says in *On Human Conduct* (1975, 8). It is in this sense that Oakeshott calls this "radically subversive" thought (*RPML* 141). It is radically subversive thought that nevertheless results in defensible conclusions.

> The aim of philosophy is to arrive at concepts which, because they presuppose nothing, are complete in themselves; the aim is to define and establish concepts so fully and so completely that nothing remains to be added. Definition is a matter of degree. All thinking is the attempt to define concepts, and philosophy is merely what occurs when thought is allowed to follow its own bent with unqualified freedom. Thought, the character of which is exemplified in every attempt at intellectual comprehension, is perfectly exemplified in philosophical comprehension (*CJP* 345).

If this is what characterizes a work as philosophical, the context of a text of political philosophy should be clear. It is the context of other works of its kind. That is, it is the context of

---

[9] At times Oakeshott identifies philosophy as a 'mood' (*EM* 2), or a 'bent of mind' (*RIP* 224).

other works that have proceeded in a philosophical manner; works that aim at a complete and unified view of the totality of experience. Though philosophy is concerned to define concepts, the emphasis is on the practice or tradition of philosophic thinking and not on the system or set of doctrines which might emerge from that thinking.

Concepts and Their Place in the History of Political Thought

The conclusions, definitions, or doctrines of a political philosopher are important in the history of political thought for Oakeshott, but mainly in their relationship to the manner in which they are determined. It is important to recall Oakeshott saw later Greeks valued pre-Socratic philosophy both as a method and as a set of conclusions or opinions and, from very early on, Oakeshott has diminished the significance of the conclusions of philosophy in favor of the practice.[10]

> For what we must know about a philosopher, if we are to understand his philosophy, is not merely *what* he thought, but also *why* he thought it. Indeed, in philosophy, this *what* and *why* are inseparable; taken apart each loses its meaning (1935a, 271).

The history of political philosophy is not merely a history of doctrines. The conclusions of philosophers are important but they are subservient to the way in which the philosopher arrived at those conclusions.

Interestingly, for Oakeshott, doctrines have their place at both the beginning and the end of philosophical contemplation. A philosophical doctrine

> should be thought of as something which happens at the end, when the concepts of science, or common-sense, or practical life are subject to the revolutionary and dissolving criticism of being related to a universal context (*CJP* 345).

But they also come in at the beginning as a definition to be interrogated in terms of its own conditionality and presuppositions. "Any genuine synthesis of 'results' must be a reinterpretation; and in interpretation what is given is accepted, not categorically as something already established, but hypotheti-

---

[10]   Socrates, a person, can become the embodiment of philosophy because philosophy has less to do with a set of doctrines than with a way of life. It was a way of life though that involved high stakes (life and death), which might distinguish it from a kind of Derridian playfulness that culminates in misology (Roochnick 1990, 163).

cally as a useful starting-place for thought". And, continuing, "if 'general philosophical principles' come in anywhere it is at the beginning and not at the end, in an examination of the presuppositions upon which these 'conclusions' rest" (*CJP* 220-21). Doctrines are incapable of being, for philosophy, groundwork upon which to build for Oakeshott. It is inadequate, therefore, to characterize the history of political thought as being united by a set of conclusions to a fixed set of questions. "It is no use looking to it for finished conclusions, for settled answers to fixed questions, because it is not a tradition of conclusions or even of questions, but of enquiry" (*CJP* 360). The focus is on the activity or practice itself and how it has developed and less on the doctrines or conclusions that may emerge from the activity.[11]

Oakeshott uses the distinction between languages and literatures to further express what he has in mind here. A language is a manner of thinking (practical, philosophical, scientific, historical) and a literature is what is said using a particular language (*RIP* 192). What is significant in a work of political philosophy is not so much the literature but the language in which it is used. If what is most valuable in the work of Aristotle are his conclusions about human biology or his conclusions about slavery, both of which today are taken to be wrong, we might be justified in no longer studying Aristotle. However, if what is most valuable is the language in which these conclusions are spoken, if it is the explanatory manner of thinking used by Aristotle to come to the conclusions he did, we may be wise to turn to Aristotle first. Even here, however, what is philosophical about Aristotle's *Politics* is a particular kind of explanatory language. In Oakeshott's LSE Lecture on Aristotle he notes the *Politics* is "best understood as a book of miscellaneous reflections on Greek political experience, the experience of polis-life", and "the reflections it contains are of many different sorts, and it begins (often without finishing) many different lines of enquiry" (Oakeshott 1960c, 78, 82).[12] However, Oakeshott continues, "[w]hat holds it together and

[11] Note how this avoids giving into the urge to define a canon of great books based on the truths they contain or to attempt to gain a cultural literacy that may be of limited value (See Bloom 1988, and Hirsch 1987).

[12] These two passages are not in the published edition of Oakeshott's LSE lectures (2006). The first passage is found in four autograph pages that preceded the typed lecture. Whether Oakeshott meant the handwritten pages as a revised, substitute introduction to this lecture is not clear. He did not make

gives it a unity is: (1) It's exclusive concern with the Greek *polis*, and (2) organization which these reflections on *polis*-life derive from having as their context [been connected with][13] Aristotle's more general understanding of the *cosmos* and the place of human beings and political activity within this *cosmos*. This, indeed, is what gives the book its philosophical character" (*LSE* 101).

What is valuable in studying the history of political philosophy is this study of explanatory languages. And, the history of what is said in these explanatory languages is "a history of the incoherencies philosophers have detected in common ways of thinking and the manner of solution they have proposed, rather than a history of doctrines and systems" (*RIP* 65). Its conclusions are mostly negative and do not relieve us of having to make choices in our own politics or of making sense of our own political experience, nor do they improve our ability to make correct political decisions. They may aid us "by removing some of the crookedness from our thinking", and may allow us "to be less often cheated by ambiguous statement and irrelevant argument", but they can offer us neither a guide to political action nor a foundation upon which to build a philosophic system.[14]

Oakeshott's and Skinner's 'Method'

Oakeshott's criteria of a masterpiece of political philosophy reveals an understanding of the activity of political philoso-

---

any marks in the typescript indicating any if it should be excised or directing one's attention to these handwritten sheets. The second passage is in the typescript but is curiously omitted from the published lectures where it would appear on page 101.

[13] The bracketed section is from the autograph version at 82. See note 12 above.

[14] What one learns from philosophy for Oakeshott has a strong parallel in Dewey's thinking, and so it is instructive to point out where the two may differ. Dewey wants free, responsible, creative individuals who are not led or misled by false thinking as well. For Dewey, however, freedom has a decidedly practical terminal point: "[t]o foresee future objective alternatives and to be able by deliberation to choose one of them and thereby weight its chances in the struggle for future existence, measures our freedom" (1974, 87). School is then not an initiation into conversation as it is for Oakeshott (more on this below), but is meant to be a microcosm of society, a training ground for the eventual struggle in society, where each child's unique gifts can be put to service: "[a]part from the thought of participation in social life the school as no end or aim"; "[t]he school cannot be a preparation for social life excepting as it reproduces, within itself, the typical conditions of social life" (1974, 114, 116).

phy that places the activity as a critical if not preeminent study in departments of politics. Oakeshott's understanding of the philosophical study of politics is not incompatible with a number of other approaches to the history of political thought and complements rather than competes with other ways of studying politics. By turning to the thoughts of another acute thinker on the history of political thought, namely Quentin Skinner, we can see how this is so.

Skinner has been remarkably consistent and reasonable in what he says the intended aims of his writings are.

> My own concern, however, has solely been with the question of how best to approach such works if our aim is, in Dunn's luminous phrase, to recover their historical identity. I have exclusively been concerned, that is, with how we should proceed if we wish to gain an understanding of the utterances that go to make up such texts, and hence an understanding of what their authors may have been saying and doing in issuing just those utterances (1988, 232).

And he argues for a methodology that promises to shed a good deal of light upon the historical meaning of political texts.

His method sets out two supremely appropriate criteria. First, one must survey the range of linguistic conventions of the time. This requires not only a careful analysis of the meaning of various words but also, importantly, the way they were used. He refers to the different ways they are used as the set of existing ideological conventions. This is the appropriate context and, Skinner says, it needs "to be treated as an ultimate framework for helping to decide what conventionally recognizable meanings, in a society of *that* kind, it might in principle have been possible for someone to have intended to communicate" ([1969] 1988, 64). He goes on to argue, quite persuasively, that starting here helps avoid a host of interpretive mistakes that lead to anachronistic interpretations or to interpretations so grossly conceived as to make it impossible for an author to have done what they are said to have done in writing the text they did.

The second criterion, which he borrows in part from the work of J.L. Austin, is to examine closely the illocutionary force of the text. That is, apart from what might have given rise to the text (or the motives of the author), to look for the 'point', or for what the author intended to do in writing what she or he wrote. Skinner makes the case that "whatever the writer is *doing in* writing what he writes must be relevant to interpretation, and thus with the claim that *amongst* the interpreter's tasks must be the recovery of the writer's intentions *in* writing what he writes" ([1976] 1988, 76).

Oakeshott's approach to the history of political thought has some marked similarities. He begins by looking at the actual utterances about politics and turns to the beliefs they may have reflected at the time. "It is these words, and the way in which they are used in political argument or in the expression of political opinions, which tell us how a people thinks when it thinks about politics" (*LSE* 40). And he sees this necessarily as a historical activity of making sense of what people have said about politics by relating it to the circumstances of its appearance or within its culture.

> What we are seeking is to understand political utterances in their place in what may be called the political culture of a people. A history of thought is a history of men thinking, *not* a 'history' of abstract disembodied 'ideas' (*LSE* 42).

So he turns to the thinking that went on at the time about politics and seeks to understand it in terms of the larger set of moral thinking of a people.

> [M]oral and political beliefs and sentiment usually develop in interaction with one another. Consequently they may be used to elucidate one another as text and context. And since our concern is with political reflection and belief, moral belief appears as the context (*MPME* 27–28).

For example, Oakeshott spends a good deal of time in his early lectures on the Greeks discussing early Greek history and focusing on the words used in politics and the meanings they had for the users. The Greek words for law are traced chronologically and shown to change meaning with changing circumstances in order to show how the Greeks understood this word and how it fit into a larger vocabulary and conception of politics.[15] There is a similar approach in Oakeshott's notebooks, where Oakeshott sees Plato critiquing the statesmen of fifth century Athens and, unlike Sparta, the lack of discipline in Athens (*Rep I*:2, 4v). Recall, part of Oakeshott's reading and

---

[15] See *LSE* 73–85. The words for law are traced from a tribal understanding of *themis* as divine insight into what is right, to *thesmos* reflecting a juridical settling of differences between conflicting *themistes* in entering into a polis, to *nomos* reflecting a more legislative and man-made character of law.

hence explanation of the meaning and force of the *Republic* is that Plato had a concern to reform Athenian democracy.

Oakeshott agrees with Skinner that the study of political thought must first be an historical study (*RIP* 63). And, he would agree, one of the important things to consider is the 'point' the author had in writing or uttering what he or she did, and that one of the best ways to do this is to locate what was said in the immediate set of circumstances and set of moral beliefs which surround what was said. This, however, is where Skinner's approach ends. Or, rather, Skinner does not make clear whether the analysis of political thought can go any further.

The impasse is occasioned by Skinner's belief that if we are talking about political thought, we must be talking about practical reflections on politics. This assumption is reflected in his treatment of what he calls the 'linguistic innovator'. The linguistic innovator's concern, according to Skinner,

> by definition is to legitimate a new range of social actions which, in terms of the existing ways of applying the moral vocabulary prevailing in his society, are currently regarded as in some way untoward or illegitimate. His aim must therefore be to show that a number of existing and favourable evaluative-descriptive terms can somehow be applied to his apparently untoward actions. If he can somehow perform this trick, he can thereby hope to argue that the condemnatory descriptions which are otherwise liable to be applied to his actions can in consequence be discounted ([1974] 1988, 112).

This, no doubt, is the character of much political discourse and particularly of that level of political thought Oakeshott identified as thought in the service of political action.[16] And Machiavelli, who Skinner is fond of using to illustrate his point, would seem a likely candidate to examine reflections of this sort.[17] Indeed it seems an adequate description of much that goes on in political debate and is an apt description of the business of an effective presidential speechwriter.

However, does this adequately describe what Dahl is doing in his book *Who Governs*? or what Hobbes is doing in *Levia-*

---

[16] See above pp. 131–133.
[17] Machiavelli wanted to ingratiate himself with the Medicis as the dedicatory letter to the *Prince* clearly reflects and he wished to rouse the people out of their political and military apathy and so aptly titles his last chapter "Exhortation to Seize Italy and to Free Her from the Barbarians" (Machiavelli 1998, 101).

than? In fact, does it describe Skinner's own reflections on the history of political thought and on particular texts in that history? Must we see Skinner's work on *The Foundations of Modern Political Thought* as the use of the linguistic opportunities available to him to persuade us into accepting his methodological approach and his political preferences? Oakeshott thinks not. As we have seen, one might see the language one uses as an attempt to describe, in the only terms available at the time, the understanding one has of one's experience. If the primary way to get leverage on what an author means is to focus on the illocutionary force of their utterances, and that force is seen primarily as an attempt to change or to maintain some ideological or linguistic convention so as to have a practical political impact, there appears to be little room for other linguistic responses. These would include at a general level explanatory responses and more specifically historical, scientific, and philosophical responses. All of which are linguistic responses different in kind to a response of the will to alter the world to achieve some imagined and wished for outcome.

Skinner glosses over some important distinctions in his aim to understand political utterances. For example, when it comes to understanding an author's intention, it is unclear whether Skinner sees a meaningful distinction between human action that is purposive and human action that is political. He seems to operate with the supposition that all action aims as reform or conservation. One may, however, aim to enjoy or to understand. He relies on a picture of human conduct that is wholly practical and narrowly utilitarian.

> To explain a voluntary action is normally to cite the end which the agent desires to bring about — corresponding to his motive for acting — together with his belief that the performance of the given action will conduce to the attainment of the desired end ([1974] 1988, 108).[18]

Or again, though one might agree we should also throw out "as an old piece of positivist bric-à-brac the alleged logical distinction between factual and evaluative statements", need this imply that all descriptions-evaluations have the intended

---

[18]   Skinner makes multiple use of the example of the policeman uttering 'the ice over there is thin', which continually points one's attention to the practical uses of language (1988, 261). His attraction to Austin is precisely because Austin argues how to *do* things with words.

force of changing or maintaining a particular set of political arrangements?

Perhaps this is too strong a critique of Skinner's intent, for despite the use (should one say deployment?) of examples of political utterances that are designed to alter or maintain political practice, Skinner may merely be announcing that it is only these *types* of political utterances that he is interested in exploring from an historian's vantage point. One wonders how compatible this is with Skinner's later claim about the proper context for understanding a political utterance. "There is no implication that the relevant context need be an immediate one", Skinner says.

> As Pocock has especially emphasized, the question and the problems to which writers see themselves as responding may have been raised at a remote period, even in a wholly different culture. The appropriate context for understanding the point of such writers' utterances will therefore be whatever context enables us to appreciate the nature of the intervention constituted by their utterances.

And, as he continues, Skinner is well aware of the potential magnitude of this undertaking: "To recover the context in any particular case, we may have to engage in extremely wide-ranging as well as extremely detailed historical research" (1988, 275).

Now if the context is this wide, it is hard to see how Skinner could be seen as engaging in the narrow historical approach to the history of political thought often attributed to him. In fact, on further reflection in a latter work, Skinner abandons his earlier rejection of 'perennial problems' in philosophy saying that his earlier statement

> appeared to deny the obvious fact that western traditions of philosophy have contained long continuities, and that these have been reflected in the stable employment of a number of key concepts and modes of argument (1988, 283).

This does not seem to place Skinner as far from, say, Leo Strauss, or Plato (or even the earlier Skinner) as it at first appears. Strauss recognized the importance of the immediate historical context for understanding a text of political philosophy and he understood there were continuing traditions of political thought—natural law traditions, natural right traditions, for example (Strauss 1950). We have seen also that Oakeshott does not ignore the historical context and equally identifies a number of traditions of political thought that give its history some continuity.[19]

When we turn to the differing beliefs about the value of studying the history of political thought (and, we have seen, what one is inclined to expect from a study of the history of political thought is deeply implicated in how that study proceeds) the real divide between Oakeshott and Skinner appears. What each sees of value in turn shows how Skinner and Oakeshott understand the very different contexts within which to make sense of political texts. Skinner makes it clear that his problem with characterizing the history of political thought as attempting to answer 'perennial questions' is only an objection to

> the practice of abstracting particular arguments from the context of their occurrence in order to relocate them as 'contributions' to such disputes. Even if we find that a given philosopher is merely reaffirming an established line of argument, we still need to be able to grasp what he or she is doing in reaffirming it if we wish to understand the argument itself (1988, 283).

It is at this point where Skinner's historical sensibility allows him to sidestep the possibility that at least some political reflections are philosophical in nature (in the Oakeshottian sense), and therefore cannot be adequately characterized as only 'interventions' or 'the deployment of a strategy' either to effect the immediate circumstantial context or a much wider historical context. Philosophy, according to Oakeshott, has no such motives to 'intervene'. Its motive is to understand, not to refute, intervene or deploy a set of ideological weapons.

It is this level of philosophical reflection on politics, this particular angle of vision Oakeshott is most interested in and which Skinner's historical sensibility blinds him to. For Oakeshott, the philosopher's motives and intent are to seek what is most complete and coherent in experience; to locate politics on the map of human activities; or, as Oakeshott characterizes it in his introduction to *Leviathan*, "[t]o establish the connections, in principle and in detail, directly or mediately, between politics and eternity" (*RIP* 225). When reflections on politics take place at this level, when reflection is radically subversive in the sense of being critical throughout, when it takes

---

[19] See especially Oakeshott's introduction to *Leviathan* (*RIP* 227–228) where he sketches what he considers to be the three great traditions of philosophical thought.

for its context the totality of experience, and when it is successful in a sufficiently complete (monistic) and detailed a manner, it rises to the level of a masterpiece of political philosophy for Oakeshott.

"Every masterpiece of political philosophy", Oakeshott says, "springs from a new vision of the predicament; each is the glimpse of a deliverance or the suggestion of a remedy" (*RIP* 226). This does not deny that different people at different times have understood the nature of this predicament differently. "[F]or the masterpiece, at least, is always the revelation of the universal predicament in the local and transitory mischief" (*RIP* 227).[20] What gives the history of political thought its unity is the pervading sense of human life as a predicament and its manner of thinking about the role of politics in human life.[21]

What is clear from Oakeshott's description of this level of political thought is that the more immediate context is not irrelevant. All reflections on politics appear in their particularity and cannot be understood without a clear understanding of their circumstantial appearance. However, philosophical reflection on politics has a timeless dimension as well in its constituent manner of thinking; in its universal aims of seeking coherence in the broadest context; in the unity of the concrete/particular and the universal/general in the unitary (monistic) whole it attempts to achieve.

---

[20] One might read this as a reformulation of the Herakleitian doctrine of 'being in becoming', or the Socratic search for a definition that subsumes all particular and partial definitions, or the Hegelian 'concrete universal'.

[21] This is not unlike Strauss's Platonic understanding of political philosophy (in "What is Political Philosophy") as "the attempt to replace opinion about the nature of political things by knowledge of the nature of political things" (Strauss 1989, 5). Oakeshott, despite many differences with Strauss (an analysis of which would take us beyond the limits of this work), agrees about the potential to go beyond immediate, common sense opinion with philosophical investigation. Oakeshott is not averse to the approach that attempts to identify *the permanent character of political activity*, as long as this "was not understood in such a manner as to suggest there is something fixed and familiar, called 'political activity', and that our knowledge of it had only to be enlarged, extended or increased in order to become philosophical knowledge" (*RPML* 151). Consider also Oakeshott's review of Strauss's book on Hobbes. Despite differences of interpretation, Oakeshott expresses admiration for Strauss's accomplishment and notes that when it comes to "what may usefully and relevantly be said about a philosophic text, Strauss's taste in this matter is faultless" (1937, 366).

For Oakeshott, though a philosopher may look to the past to see what others may have said, and may even draw on what has been said in the past because it helps fully illuminate one's own experience, in the end the criteria brought to bear on the value of what reflections survive from the past is their logical value and not just their historical value. The philosopher, in Oakeshott's view, may begin with an historical study to understand what a philosopher has said, but in determining the value of what is said the historian's criteria of time and place are irrelevant (*EM* 349). This is precisely how Oakeshott treated the pre-Socratics in his notebooks. What counted as an advance was a logical advance and not a chronological advance.

When we turn to what Skinner's thoughts on the value of the study of the history of ideas, he tells us, it is "the possibility of a dialogue between philosophical discussion and historical evidence"; it may help us gain insight into how languages change, into the relationship between belief and action, and into the sociology of knowledge ([1969] 1988, 64). However, Skinner never spells out how this dialogue is possible. The question of how languages change is not a philosophical question. It is an historical question, if it is approached at the level of how *this particular language* changed. Or a scientific question, if one brings to the table the supposition that languages change according to some regular pattern (something Skinner is critical of in other historians of ideas). The relationship between belief and action may be a philosophic question, but then it is a logical question and not one the philosopher would pursue by collecting evidence from the past to somehow deduce this relationship.

Skinner is clearer in his later writings what he sees of value in a study of the history of political thought: it can give us some critical distance on our own culture; we might find that what we believe is false; by seeing the "changing applications of our key concepts, it will also enable us to uncover the points at which they may have become confused or misunderstood in a way that marked their subsequent history" or, it may help "to dissolve some of our current philosophical perplexities" (1988, 286-88). How this can emerge from an historical study of the past is not at all apparent. What seems to be required to elicit this from the past is something other than an historical attitude. In order to conclude from such a study of the history of political thought that what we believe is false, or to see where a concept became confused or misunderstood, is to bring a practical set of considerations to the past neither the historian *qua* historian nor the philosopher *qua* philosopher is interested in. Further, this belief reflects Skinner's proclivity for placing the emphasis on the set of conclusions reached by a particular thinker on the *obiter dicta* and to treat the *ratio decidendi* as merely the instrument to that end. This is what allows him to declare "concepts are tools", and to adopt a contradictory set of beliefs about the history of political thought. On the one hand, in a manner reminiscent of Mill, this history may help us to dissolve some of our current philosophical perplexities, to help us critically evaluate our own culture where we might find out what we believe is false. On the other hand (and Skinner might have done well to stick with this more skeptical position),

> whenever it is claimed that the point of the historical study of such questions [that is timeless ones] is that we may learn directly from the *answers*, it will be found that what *counts* as an answer will usually look, in a different culture or period, so different in itself that it can hardly be in the least helpful even to go on thinking of the relevant question as being 'the same' in the required sense at all. More crudely: we must do our own thinking for ourselves ([1969] 1988, 66).

It may be true that the history of political thought shows us the inescapable parameters within which we must choose to act, but can it actually help us choose more correctly? But again, it is the emphasis on the answers and conclusions of philosophical reflections on politics that leads Skinner to this conclusion. And this conclusion naturally leads one to wonder why anyone other than someone interested in the past for its own sake might study the history of political thought.

Oakeshott does not end up where Skinner does. Rather, by articulating clearly the different kinds of political reflection likely found in a political text, Oakeshott is able to both acknowledge the important role that the historical study of political thought has to play and to move beyond it. If the study of political thought were only an historical study; if the only thing one hopes to find in a set of reflections on politics is an engagement in politics (that is a set of *practical* reflections on politics); the books of the past do become merely time-bound and not interesting except for the historian—they do "fade into the landscape" (Saxonhouse 1993, 3).

However, if the historical reflection gives way to the philosophical reflection on texts from the past, something of different significance might be had. By understanding political texts in a larger philosophic context what is revealed in the history of political thought is a tradition of enquiry, Oakeshott insists. It is a tradition that attempts to make sense of the character of politics, of the relationship of politics to other human activities, and of the relationship of politics to eternity. Oakeshott had a continuing concern to preserve this tradition, this "living, extemporary whole in which past and present are comparatively insignificant" (1937, 359) not because it contains a set of truths revealed by a group of authors, but because it reveals, in a set of concrete and profound reflections, different manners (or levels) of thinking. It is by acquainting ourselves with these manners of thinking that we become more critical and discriminating about our own politics and ourselves, and become less likely to be misled by irrelevant argument.

The philosophical investigation of politics is not something less rigorous than other investigations of politics. It is a critical historical and philosophical enquiry. Its rigor and meaningfulness are not diminished, for Oakeshott, because it cannot guide our practical political reflections. Oakeshott's view of the history of political thought deflates the pretension that the power philosophical investigation is supposed to afford: discovering the 'foundations', laying out the fundamental principle upon which to build, discovering the ultimate truth to guide one's actions, showing us the demonstrably correct political choice to make. It is none of these, despite the promise Plato may have made.[22]

---

[22]   A recent issue of *Political Theory* shows a kind of anxiety among very different political theorists that rigor and meaningfulness is lost when political theory does not produce practical political insight. George Kateb laments that the 'canon' does not, did not in the case of twentieth century atrocities, provide a lesson. Adriana Cavarero, following Arendt, is concerned that political theory is too otherworldly, radically separating the *vita contemplativa* from the *vita activa* despite the fact she believes political theory does not coincide with politics. James Tully, following Skinner, maps political theory onto practical politics insisting political philosophers are "not doing anything different in *kind* from the citizens involved in argumentation" (544). Ruth Grant sees political theory as an extension of political thinking itself and not different in kind. And, Ian Shapiro, despite his sensitivity to contingency, opts for a practical cri-

The philosophical study of the history of political thought is not practical political thinking in the usual sense, but it is, nevertheless, more than an idiosyncratic interest in timeless questions. It is the attempt to make the most sense of politics for ourselves by seeing what others have had to say about the matter and reflecting in as profound a manner, in as large a context, in as subversive a way as they have.

To return to Hobbes's *Leviathan*, what makes this work a masterpiece for Oakeshott is Hobbes's courage to maintain a philosophic mood.

> The coherence of his philosophy, the system of it, lies not in an architectonic structure, but in a single 'passionate thought' that pervades its parts . . . And the thread, the hidden thought, is the continuous application of a doctrine about the nature of philosophy . . . Hobbes's philosophy is the world reflected in the mirror of the philosophic eye, each image the representation of a fresh object, but each determined by the character of the mirror itself (*RIP* 236).

The mirror is a mirror of energetic and systematic reasoning about causes, moved by doubt and skeptical of reliance on faith, empiricism, or prudential experience in the "perpetual re-establishment of coherence" (*RIP* 237-41, 231).

In this effort to maintain a manner of thinking that is critical throughout, Oakeshott implies in his LSE Lectures and in his personal notebooks, Hobbes succeeded better than others. Despite Oakeshott's characterization of Plato's *Republic* as another masterpiece, he also characterizes it in his notebook, as we have seen, as a book of moral philosophy (*Rep I*:1). As such, it falls short of its philosophic character by limiting it to the context of practical experience or by qualifying thought in some say. In *Experience and Its Modes*, Oakeshott calls this an 'arrest in experience', and in his first course of lectures at Cambridge he calls it 'pseudo-philosophical thinking' or thinking "which has failed to go far enough" (*EM* 345; *CL* VII:1).[23] As we

---

terion to judge better and worse explanations and the ability to predict (*Political Theory* vol. 30, no. 4).

[23] As indicated earlier, the content of these lectures is in many ways a lecture version of *Experience and Its Modes*, and contains themes on the nature of philosophy that Oakeshott works out in his essays that follow these works: "The Concept of a Philosophical Jurisprudence" (*CJP* 1938), "The Concept of a Philosophy of Politics" (*RPML* 119ff.), and "Political Philosophy" (*RPML* 138ff.). This adds weight to Paul Franco's approach to *Experience and Its Modes* as a work predominantly concerned about philosophy, though not necessarily that it

have seen, Plato was following the philosophic path of pursuing thought that is critical throughout but he falls short in taking refuge in the comfort of imperatives ('the good', 'ought', 'why should I be moral?') without attempting to transform these into indicatives.[24]

Leviathan achieves this level of reflection more thoroughly.[25] In Oakeshott's inimitable language, we discover in *Leviathan* "the true character of a masterpiece — the still centre of a whirlpool of ideas which has drawn into itself numberless currents of thought, contemporary and historic, and by its centripetal force has shaped and compressed them into a momentary significance before they are flung off again into the future" (*RIP* 228).

While I have been primarily concerned to elucidate this significance in terms of the history of political thought, there is another way Oakeshott identifies *Leviathan's* significance. *Leviathan* is significant not only for its philosophic character but for its poetic character. From a different point of view, the power of Hobbes's imagination manifested itself in the creation of a myth, according to Oakeshott. "*Leviathan* is a myth, the transposition of an abstract argument into the world of the imagination. In it we are made aware at a glance of the fixed and simple centre of a universe of complex and changing relationships". It is "an accomplishment of art that Hobbes, in the history of political philosophy, shares only with Plato" (*RIP* 234–35). This last thought points to a fundamental concern Oakeshott had in distinguishing different modes of experience, different languages of explanation, and different levels of political reflection. That concern is to conserve the poetic element in life, a concern analyzed further in the concluding chapter.

---

represents Oakeshott's response on task of philosophy in an age of science (1990, 13–14).

[24] This is Oakeshott's vocabulary that he uses in multiple places to describe the character of philosophic thought as critical throughout and primarily descriptive in nature (*CJP* 350; *RPML* 130–31).

[25] This direct comparison between Plato and Hobbes as philosophers was provoked by Timothy Fuller's comment to me that Oakeshott's LSE Lectures can be seen as a debate between Plato and Hobbes where Hobbes turns out to be the better philosopher.

Chapter VII

Conclusion

The original impetus that animated this work was to attempt to think through what we are doing when we are engaging in political philosophy; to understand and explain the significance of having students read, study, and discuss a book like Plato's *Republic* or Hobbes's *Leviathan*. Oakeshott helps us answer these important questions by offering an alternative he believes is part of a tradition reaching back to the beginning of philosophical thought. A unique opportunity for understanding more fully the depth and significance of Oakeshott's answer was made possible by the availability of his notebooks on ancient Greek political thought. Through an analysis of what Oakeshott found important in some of these earliest of thinkers we were able to see how different components of his thinking fit together into a general approach to the study of the history of political thought.

Oakeshott understood the philosophical study of politics to have a history of its own. This history began with the pre-Socratic poets' doubt and skepticism about traditional sources of authority; with a turn away from accepting traditional, mythological explanations and toward rational attempts to interpret and understand the world. This attempt was deliberately pursued with Thales and refined as the attempt to find the underlying unity in variety by searching for the single material underlying all the apparent diversity. These early attempts were rejected by the Sophists of fifth century Athens for leading to dead ends and for being useless for getting on in life and politics. The Sophists focused their attention on practical, social and political concerns. Oakeshott understands Socrates to return to a more detached perspective of the pre-Socratic physiologists but seeking a "spiritual" or ideational not a material unity. Though keeping the focus on the social and the political, Socrates separates practical con-

cerns and philosophical ones, and in doing so is understood by
Oakeshott as a practical conservative but a philosophical radical. Plato had too much of the reformer in him to follow faithfully the line that Socrates suggested, and Plato's influence
continues to be seen in contemporary understandings of the
state and of the study of politics. Oakeshott thought philosophy had come to be by the eighteenth century a practice that
could be understood, much like art in the modern age, largely
released from practical concerns and engaged in for its own
sake. Many thinkers in the history of political thought had
achieved high levels of critical detachment and had pursued
the engagement to understand politics' place on the larger
map of human experience. Those who submitted more fully to
the impulse of all thinking, to pursue rational coherence,
wherever it may lead, are ones we can learn most from, according to Oakeshott.

What is it precisely that we are to learn, let alone teach, from
these masterpieces? There is a lot Oakeshott sees as incidental
and not the central focus of the engagement with these works.
One does not gain some kind of practical guidance on the
burning political questions of the day. Nor does one learn a
failsafe technique for approaching contemporary political
questions (only a Sophist, Oakeshott says, would consider the
most significant thing to be learned to be a "separate *techne*"
(*VLL* 126).) A persistent concern of Oakeshott, one that weaves
its way through his notebooks and his published work, is to
keep philosophy separate from practical activity, but not to
place one over the other.[1] As Oakeshott says in *Experience and
Its Modes*:

> A man cannot be a philosopher and nothing else; to be so were
> either more or less than human. Such a life would, indeed, be at
> once febrile and insipid and not to be endured. But in philosophy
> (seldom desired and less often achieved), what is satisfactory is

[1]   There is an interesting contrast with Collingwood here who, in *Speculum Men-
      tis*, also "set out to construct a map of knowledge on which every legitimate
      form of human experience should be laid down, its boundaries determined,
      and its relations with it neighbors set forth" (1924, 306). Collingwood identi-
      fies a number of dominant experiences as more or less mutually exclusive,
      autonomous 'modes' of experience (art, religion, science, history, and philoso-
      phy). One of the central differences with Oakeshott is that for Collingwood
      there is a *progress* in thinking that culminates in philosophy, which is under-
      stood as 'absolute knowledge' for Collingwood. For Oakeshott, each mode
      does not build upon another progressively, yet philosophy, though not the sci-
      ence of sciences, has a rather peculiar, parasitic standing among these modes.

only what is positive and complete. And when philosophy is sought, it must be for its own sake. It depends for its existence upon maintaining its independence from all extraneous interests, and in particular from the practical interest (*EM* 3).

This is hardly the Platonic desire to be released once and for all from desire and change into a realm of unchanging being; to have one's soul be wholly subsumed by reason. But, if practical concerns are not to be despised but are not the aim of the activity of philosophy, what is the aim? And, why might it be pursued for its own sake?

The aim, as we have seen, is to find that monistic unity or coherence in thought, to achieve a satisfactory explanation of some phenomena, like politics, by establishing its place on the larger map of human experience. One begins with common opinions, or what is taken to the character and place of politics, which like Cephalus' understanding, is not devoid of meaning and knowledge. The activity is to identify incoherence in our thoughts and seek a better definition or understanding. Oakeshott characterizes the process as fundamentally a Socratic one in his notebooks and elsewhere. In an interesting book review of R.G. Collingwood's *Principles of Art* in 1938, Oakeshott praises the author's pursuit of the Socratic method, which he characterizes in the following way:

> First, without any suggestion of a theory, he tries to disentangle what as a matter of fact, we all know about art, in the belief that the truth is to be found *in* what we all know about it, thought often the truth is not exactly what we at first take it to be. This leaves us with a number of philosophical questions to be investigated, because in stating what we all know about art we make use of words and expressions — sensation, thought, emotion, language — which call for analysis. Lastly, there comes the construction of a Theory of Art, a synthesis of the truths which have emerged and established themselves in the earlier discussions ([1938] 1970, 140).

The activity is a dialectical one of examining opinions (which contain some truth) and, through criticism and rejection, of bringing more coherence to our ideas of our experience. It involves a kind of Socratic reminiscence: "knowledge is always the getting to know more fully something that is already known", Oakeshott says in *Experience and Its Modes* (1933, 348). It is critical throughout in its use of dialectic, but its aim is to seek a kind of 'being.' It is a 'being,' however, that is immanent in experience not separate and beyond everyday experience in some mystical realm. As Oakeshott puts it, "the permanent *it* is what it *becomes* when given a place in an intelligible universe" (1933, 151).

Philosophy is, however, a rather peculiar activity in its radical skepticism.

> Philosophy is particular merely because, in the pursuit of this process [of coming to understand more fully] it is governed by a radical scepticism with regard to every stopping place that is suggested; it is suspicious of every attempt to limit the enquiry (*EM* 348).

Other modes, voices, or standpoints are different in that they are defined, limited, and achieve their perfection by adhering to a set of assumptions (e.g., in science for example the assumption is that particular phenomena are examples of some more generalized process or set of laws). Human beings have developed a number of separate and autonomous perspectives from which to understand the world. Collectively they constitute a distinctive culture. Individually these modes or perspectives Oakeshott identifies, in one of his most memorable images in a speech on education, as voices in a conversation.

> Perhaps we may think of these components of a culture as voices, each the expression of a distinct and conditional understanding of the world and a distinct idiom of human self-understanding, and of the culture itself as these voices joined, as such voices could only be joined, in a conversation—an endless unrehearsed intellectual adventure in which, in imagination, we enter into a variety of modes of understanding the world and ourselves and are not disconcerted by the differences or dismayed by the inconclusiveness of it all. And perhaps we may recognize liberal learning as, above all else, an education in imagination, an initiation into the art of this conversation in which we learn to recognize the voices; to distinguish their different modes of utterance, to acquire the intellectual and moral habits appropriate to this conversational relationship and thus to make our *début dans la vie humaine* (*VLL* 38–39).

The aim of this activity, philosophy, is then to understand and explain some particular activity or phenomena by locating it on the map of human experience as a whole, a map that is rich with understandings and activities. Philosophy is engaging in a rather eccentric activity that is part of this collective experience we call one's culture or tradition. "The impulse to study the quality and style of each voice, and to reflect upon the relationship of one voice to another, must be counted a parasitic activity; it springs from the conversation, because it is what the philosopher reflects upon, but it makes no specific contribution to it" (*RIP* 491). This raises the question, again, why should this activity be pursued?

The answer Oakeshott gives to the question of why philosophy might be pursued and why it might be an end in itself, is inseparable from the diagnosis Oakeshott has of the direction this conversation has taken — a direction he diagnoses early in his notebooks. An abiding concern of Oakeshott's was to preserve and restore the richness, the variety, and the sense of wonder that this conversation embodies and evokes. Oakeshott is worried that some voices in this conversation are or will be overshadowed by others, and the conversation has or will become boring by degenerating into an argument or a monologue. A threat Oakeshott identified early in his notebooks was the voice of practice, and so, as we saw, he took great pains to identify the philosophical activity as separate from practice, without diminishing or attempting to reform existing practice through his reading of Socrates. In Oakeshott's ambivalent relationship to Plato and in his identification of different levels of political reflection, a major concern is to secure practical concerns as separate and distinct from theoretical ones. In a later essay, published posthumously, Oakeshott calls the dominance of the practical voice as 'deadly' (1995, 33).

Oakeshott's anxiety is that life would be rather pale and insipid if at bottom life were "a perpetual and restless desire of power after power, that ceaseth only in death." Oakeshott is grateful human beings have created, though accident and choice, different ways of understanding the world and engaging in the world that have nothing to do with power, success, change, conservation, hope, desire, action, aversion, etc. The world today, Oakeshott says in a later essay entitled "A Place of Learning" has but one language, "the language of appetite" (*VLL* 41). One recalls Polemarchus in reading Oakeshott's description of a contemporary culture that diminishes all reflections, save those instrumental to action.

> From an early age children now believe themselves to be well-informed about the world, but they know it only second-hand in the pictures and voices that surround them. It holds no puzzles or mysteries for them; it invites neither careful attention nor understanding. As like as not they know the moon as

> something to be shot at or occupied before ever they have had the
> chance to marvel at it (*VLL* 41).

Philosophy like science, when it is not approached as a method
for better living through technology, like history, when it is not
mined for moral lessons or political guidance, and like art and
music, offers a response to the world that is as valuable as a
practical response; and a response worth preserving in the face
of eclipse by practical concerns. A central concern of
Oakeshott is to re-establish civility among the voices in this
conversation by showing the limits, but also the contributions
and dignity of each voice.

In Oakeshott's most skeptical moments he insists this conversation is all we have. That this "world of understandings,
imaginings, meanings, moral and religious beliefs, relationships, practices — states of mind in which the human condition
is to be discerned as recognitions of and responses to the
ordeal of consciousness" is all there is (*VLL* 93). We enter into
this conversation as soon as we arrive upon the scene and
begin to learn to make our way about the world. The learning
component it is worth emphasizing again is critical for
Oakeshott. In fact, we cannot help but learn as human beings.

> These states of mind can be entered into only by being themselves
> understood, and they can be understood only by learning to do
> so. To be initiated into this world is learning to become human;
> and to move within it freely is being human, which is an 'historic,'
> not a 'natural' condition (*VLL* 93).

Cephalus comes to mind here — the meaning(s) of the world
Cephalus has learned by living and participating in the world.
There is, however, a separate practice wholly devoted to
understanding the world, a world made far more diverse and
complex because of the interval within which to have and
record new responses to this 'ordeal of consciousness.'

We are condemned to be learners for Oakeshott because the
world is a world of meanings. We can only enter this world by
learning the meanings others have constructed and by making
sense of these meanings for ourselves. Much of this learning
takes place along the way as we adventure through our lives.
This is genuine knowledge of the world Oakeshott maintains
(against Plato) as is revealed through his treatment of
Cephalus and his reading of the Platonic Forms. However,
human beings have devoted specific places (universities)

where learning about this world of meanings is intentional and its sole objective.

Reading a book like the *Republic* is a deliberate attempt to learn more about this world of meanings that we inherit and to do so without any loss or sacrifice to getting on in the world. The greatest gift of university education Oakeshott identifies is what he calls the 'gift of the interval' (*VLL* 101, 127). And he describes it in the following manner:

> Here was an opportunity to put aside the hot allegiances of youth without the necessity of acquiring new loyalties to take their place. Here was an interval in which a man might refuse to commit himself. Here was a break in the tyrannical course of irreparable events; a period in which to look round upon the world without the sense of an enemy at one's back or the insistent pressure to make up one's mind; a moment in which one was relieved of the necessity of 'coming to terms with oneself' or of entering the fiercely trivial partisan struggles of the world outside; a moment in which to taste the mystery without the necessity of at once seeking a solution. Here, indeed, was an opportunity to exercise, and perhaps to cultivate, the highest and most easily destroyed of human capacities, what Keats called 'negative capability' — 'when a man is capable of being in uncertainties, mysteries, doubts, without any irritable racing after fact and reason' — an opportunity to practice that 'suspended judgement' of which the 'neutrality' of liberalism is so pale a shadow (*VLL* 127).

Reading a book like Plato's *Republic* with students, then, is a deliberate transaction between students and teacher to initiate students, not into some set of doctrines, but into a conversation that was begun long ago when a group of human beings were free enough from practical matters to develop other ways of thinking and being active in the world. Plato made a memorable contribution to the conversation. By entering into the imaginative world of Plato, we are provoked and challenged to reflect upon our own assumptions, to reflect upon our own understandings and to develop our own unique voices, and become conversational partners in the conversation of mankind.

Bibliography

Acton, John Emerich Edward. [1907] 1967. *Historical Essays and Studies*. Reprint Edition. Edited by John Neville Figgis and Reginald Vere Laurence. Freeport, NY: Books for Libraries Press, Inc.

Aliotta, Antonio. 1914. *The Idealist Reaction Against Science*. Translated by Agnes McCaskill. London: Macmillan and Co.

Arendt, Hannah. 1958. *The Human Condition*. Chicago and London: University of Chicago Press.

Aristotle. 1961. *Metaphysics*. Translated by John Warrington. London: J.M. Dent and Sons, Ltd.; New York: E.P. Dutton and Co., Inc.

— 1984. *Politics*. Translated by Carnes Lord. Chicago and London: University of Chicago Press.

Austin, J.L. 1975. *How to Do Things With Words*. Cambridge, MA: Harvard University Press.

Barker, Ernest. 1906. *The Political Thought of Plato and Aristotle*. London: Methuen & Co.

— [1918] 1957. *Greek Political Theory: Plato and His Predecessors*. London: Methuen & Co.

Berkeley, George. 1871. *The Works of George Berkeley*. Collected and Edited with Prefaces and Annotations by Alexander Campbell Fraser. Vol. II. Oxford: Clarendon Press.

Bloom, Allan. 1968. *The Republic of Plato*. Second Edition. Translated with Notes and an Interpretative Essay by Allan Bloom. New York: Basic Books.

— 1988. *The Closing of the American Mind*. Touchstone Edition. New York, London, Toronto, Sydney, Tokyo and Singapore: Simon and Schuster.

Bosanquet, Bernard. 1906. *A Companion to Plato's Republic for English Readers Being a Commentary adapted to Davies and Vaughan's Translation*. Second Edition. London: Rivington's.

— 1917. *The Education of the Young in* The Republic *of Plato*. Translated with notes and introduction. Cambridge: Cambridge University Press.

— 1923. *The Philosophical Theory of the State*. Fourth edition. London: Macmillan and Co.

Boucher, David. 1985. *Texts in Context: Revisionist Methods for Studying the History of Ideas*. Dordrecht, Boston, and Lancaster: Martinus Nijhoff Publishers.

— 1997. *The British Idealists*. Cambridge: Cambridge University Press.

— 2000. *British Idealism & Political Theory*. Edinburgh: Edinburgh University Press.

Bradley, Francis H. 1897. *Appearance and Reality*. Second Edition. Oxford: Clarendon Press.

— 1962. *Ethical Studies*. Second, Paperback Edition. Oxford: Oxford University Press.

— 1993. *The Presuppositions of Critical History* and *Aphorisms*. Reprint Edition. Bristol: Thoemmes Press.

Burke, Edmund. [1790] 1955. *Reflections on the Revolution in France*. Edited by Thomas H.D. Mahoney. Indianapolis and New York: Bobbs-Merrill Company, Inc.

Burnet, John. 1908. *Early Greek Philosophy*. Second Edition. London: Adam & Charles Black.

— [1914] 1964. *Greek Philosophy: Thales to Plato*. London: Macmillan & Co. Ltd.; New York: St. Martin's Press.

Bush, George W. 2002. State of the Union Address. Reprinted in *The New York Times*. 30 January. A22.

Cavarero, Adriana. 2002. "Politicizing Theory". *Political Theory* 30(4):506–532.

Coats, John Wendell. 2000. *Oakeshott and His Contemporaries: Montaigne, St. Augustine, Hegel, et al*. Selinsgroves: Susquehanna University Press; London: Associated University Presses.

Collingwood, R.G. 1924. *Speculum Mentis or The Map of Knowledge*. Oxford: Clarendon Press.

Covell, Charles. 1986. *The Redefinition of Conservatism*. Houndsmills, Basingstoke, Hamphsire RG21 2XS, and London: Macmillan Press.

Dahl, Robert A. 1961. *Who Governs?* New Haven and London: Yale University Press.

Davies, John Llewelyn and David James Vaughan, Translators. 1902. *The Republic of Plato*. A.L. Burt Company, Publishers.

Den Otter, Sandra M. 1996. *British Idealism and Social Explanation: A Study in Late Victorian Thought*. Oxford: Clarendon Press.

Devigne, Robert. 1994. *Recasting Conservativism: Oakeshott, Strauss, and the Response to Postmodernism*. New Haven and London: Yale University Press.

Dewey, John. 1974. "Human Nature and Conduct". In *John Dewey and Education: Selected Writings*. Edited by Reginald D. Archambault. University of Chicago Edition. Chicago and London: University of Chicago Press.

Erdmann, Johann Eduard. 1890. *A History of Philosophy*. Vol. 1. Translated by Williston S. Hough. London: Swan Sonnenschein& Co.

Ewing, Alfred C. 1957. *The Idealist Tradition from Berkeley to Blanshard*. Glencoe, IL: The Free Press.

Farr, Anthony. 1998. *Sarte's Radicalism and Oakeshott's Conservatism*. London: Macmillan Press Ltd.; New York: St. Martin's Press, Inc.

Ferrier, James Frederick. 1866. *Lectures on Greek Philosophy and Other Philosophical Remains*. Edinburgh and London: William Blackwood & Sons.

Foster, Michael B. [1935] 1965. *The Political Philosophies of Plato and Hegel*. Reissued Edition. New York: Russell & Russell.

Francis, Mark and John Morrow. 1994. *A History of English Political Thought in the Nineteenth Century*. London: Gerald Duckworth & Co. Ltd.

Franco, Paul. 1990. *The Political Philosophy of Michael Oakeshott*. New Haven and London: Yale University Press.

Freeman, Kathleen. 1953. *The Pre-Socratic Philosophers: A Companion to Diels*, Fragmente der Vorsokratiker. Third Edition. Oxford: Basil Blackwell.

— 1966. *Ancilla to The Pre-Socratic Philosophers: A Complete Translation of the Fragments in Diels*, Fragmente der Vorsokratiker. Cambridge: Harvard University Press.

Gadamer, Hans-Georg. 1998. *The Beginning of Philosophy*. Translated by Rod Coltman. New York: Continuum Publishing Company.

Gerencser, Steven Anthony. 2000. *The Skeptic's Oakeshott*. New York: St. Martin's Press.

Gordon, Peter and John White. 1979. *Philosophers as Educational Reformers: The Influence of Idealism on British Educational Thought and Practice*. London, Boston, and Henley: Routledge & Kegan Paul.

Grant, Robert. 1990. *Oakeshott*. London: The Claridge Press.

Grant, Ruth W. 2002. "Political Theory, Political Science, and Politics". *Political Theory* 30(4):577–595.

Green, Thomas Hill. 1886. *Works of Thomas Hill Green*. Vol. II: "Philosophical Works". Edited by R.L. Nettleship. London: Longmans, Green, and Co.

Greenleaf, W.H. 1966. *Oakeshott's Philosophical Politics*. New York: Barns & Noble Inc.

Gunnell, John G. 1978. "The Myth of the Tradition". *American Political Science Review* 72(1):122–134.

Hegel, Georg Wilhelm Friedrich. [1892] 1963. *Lectures on the History of Philosophy*. Translated by E.S. Haldane. Reprint edition. Vol. 1. London: Routledge & Kegan Paul; New York: The Humanities Press.

— 1894. *Lectures on the History of Philosophy*. Translated by E.S. Haldane and Frances H. Simon. Vol. 2. London: Kegan Paul, Tranch, Trübner & Co., Ltd.

Hirsch, E.D. 1987. *Cultural Literacy: What Every American Needs to Know*. Boston: Houghton Mifflin Company.

Honig, Bonnie and David R. Mapel. 2002. *Skepticism, Individuality, and Freedom: The Reluctant Liberalism of Richard Flathman*. Minneapolis and London: University of Minnesota Press.

Jacobs, David C. *The Presocratics After Heidegger*. New York: New York State University Press.

Jowett, Benjamin. 1888. Introduction to Plato's *Republic*. Translated by B. Jowett. Third Edition. Oxford: Clarendon Press.

Kateb, George. 2002. "The Adequacy of the Canon". *Political Theory* 30(4):482–505.

King, Preston and B.C. Parekh. 1968. *Politics and Experience: Essays Presented to Professor Michael Oakeshott on the Occasion of his Retirement*. Cambridge: Cambridge University Press.

Lutoslawski, Wincenty. 1897. *The Origin and Growth of Plato's Logic, with an account of Plato's style and of the chronology of his writings*. London, New York and Bombay: Longmans, Green, and Co.

Machiavelli, Niccolò. 1998. *The Prince*. Translated by Harvey C. Mansfield. Second Edition. Chicago and London: University of Chicago Press.

MacIntyre, Alasdair. 1990. *Three Rival Versions of Moral Inquiry: Encyclopaedia, Genealogy, and Tradition*. Notre Dame: University of Notre Dame Press.

McTaggart, John McTaggart Ellis. 1895. "The Necessity of Dogma". *International Journal of Ethics*. 5(2):147–162.

— 1906. *Some Dogmas of Religion*. London: Edward Arnold.

— 1934. "Mysticism". In *Philosophical Studies*. Edited by S.V. Keeling. London: Edward Arnold & Co. Originally published in *The New Quarterly* II(7)(1909):315–39.

Minogue, Kenneth. 1993. Introduction to *Morality and Politics in Modern Europe: The Harvard Lectures*. Edited by Shirley Robin Letwin. New Haven and London: Yale University Press.

Muirhead, John N. [1931] 1992. *The Platonic Tradition in Anglo-Saxon Philosophy: Studies in the History of Idealism in England and America*. Reprint Edition. Bristol: Thoemmes Press. Originally published, London: George Allen & Unwin Ltd.

Nardin, Terry. 2001. *The Philosophy of Michael Oakeshott*. University Park, PA: Pennsylvania State University Press.

Nettleship, Richard Lewis. 1897. *Philosophical Lectures and Remains*. Two Volumes. Edited by A.C. Bradley and G.R. Benson. London: Macmillan and Co.

— [1880] 1906. *The Theory of Education in the Republic of Plato*. Chicago: Univeristy of Chicago Press. Originally published in *Hellenica: A Collection of Essays on Greek Poetry, Philosophy, History, and Religion*. Edited by Evelyn Abbott. London: Rivingtons.

Newman, W.L. 1887 and 1902. *The Politics of Aristotle, with and Introduction, Two Prefatory Essays and Notes Critical and Explanatory*. Four Volumes. Oxford: Clarendon Press.

Nicholson, Peter P. 1990. *The Political Philosophy of the British Idealists*. Cambridge: Cambridge University Press.

Norman, Jesse. 1993. *The Achievement of Michael Oakeshott*. London: Gerald Duckworth & Co, Ltd.

Oakeshott, Michael J. October [1923] 1925. Notebook titled *Early Greek Philosophy*. London School of Economics and Political Science, Archive reference 2/4/1.

— July 1923. Notebooks titled *Republic I* and *Republic II*. London School of Economics and Political Science, Archive reference 2/2/1 and 2/2/2.

— 1931c. Lectures titled *The Philosophical Approach to Politics*. London School of Economics and Political Science, Archive reference 1/1/7.

— 1933. *Experience and Its Modes*. Cambridge: Cambridge University Press.

— 1935a. "Thomas Hobbes". *Scrutiny* IV(3):263–277.

— 1935b. Review of M.B. Foster's *The Political Philosophies of Plato and Hegel*. *Cambridge Review* 57(1934–35):248.

— 1937. "Dr. Leo Strauss on Hobbes". *Politica* 2:364–379.

— [1937] 1975. *Hobbes on Civil Association*. Indianapolis: Liberty Fund, Inc.

— 1938. "The Concept of a Philosophical Jurisprudence". *Politica* 3:203–222, 345–360.

— [1938] 1970. Review of R.G. Collingwood's *Principles of Art*. *Cambridge Review*, 59(1937–8):487. Reprinted in *The Cambridge Mind: Ninety Years of the* Cambridge Review, *1879–1969*. London: Jonathan Cape.

— 1946. Introduction to *Leviathan*. Oxford: Basil Blackwell.

— 1947. "The 'Collective Dream of Civilization'". *The Listener* 37:966–67.

— 1952. Review of *Two Cheers for Democracy*, by E.M. Forester. *Cambridge Journal* V(1951–52):436–438.

— 1960c. Lectures titled *A Study of Political Thought: A Series of Lectures by Michael Oakeshott*. London School of Economics and Political Science, Archive reference 1/1/21.

— 1975. *On Human Conduct*. Oxford: The Clarendon Press.

— 1989. *The Voice of Liberal Learning*. Edited by Timothy Fuller. New Haven and London: Yale University Press.

— 1991. *Rationalism in Politics and Other Essays*. New and Expanded edition with a forward by Timothy Fuller. Indianapolis: Liberty Fund. Originally published London and New York: Methuen and Co. Ltd.

— 1993a. *Religion, Politics and the Moral Life*. Edited by Timothy Fuller. New Haven and London: Yale University Press.

— 1993b. *Morality and Politics in Modern Europe: The Harvard Lectures*. Edited by Shirley Robin Letwin with and introduction by Kenneth Mingoue. New Haven and London: Yale University Press.

— 1995. "Work and Play". *First Things*. June/July, No. 54:29–33.

— 2004. *What is History? And Other Essays*. Edited by Luke O'Sullivan. Exeter, UK and Charlottesville, VA: Imprint Academic.

— 2006. *Lectures in the History of Political Thought*. Edited by Terry Nardin and Luke O'Sullivan. Exeter, UK and Charlottesville, VA: Imprint Academic.

O'Sullivan, Luke. 2003. *Oakeshott on History*. Exeter and Charlottesville, VA: Imprint Academics.

Pater, Walter. 1893. *Plato and Platonism: A Series of Lectures*. New York and London: Macmillan & Co.

Plato. 1956. *Philebus and Epinomis*. Translated with an introduction by A.E. Taylor. Edited by Raymond Klibansky, with cooperation of Guido Cologero and A.C. Lloyd. London, Edinburgh, Paris, Melbourne, Toronto, and New York: Thomas Nelson and Sons, Ltd.

— 1968. *The Republic of Plato*. Second Edition. Translated with Notes and an Interpretative Essay by Allan Bloom. New York: Basic Books.

— 1975. *Apology*. In *The Trial and Death of Socrates*. Translated by G.M.A. Grube. Indianapolis, IN: Hackett Publishing Co, Inc.

— 1975. *Crito*. In *The Trial and Death of Socrates*. Translated by G.M.A. Grube. Indianapolis, IN: Hackett Publishing Co, Inc.

— 1987. *Gorgias*. Translated by Donald J. Zeyl. Indianapolis, IN: Hackett Publishing Co.

— 1987. *Theaetetus*. Translated with and Essay by Robin A. H. Waterfield. New York and London: Penguin Books.

Quinton, A.M. 1971. "Absolute Idealism". In *Proceedings of the British Academy*, LVII:303–329.

Reese, William L. 1980. *Dictionary of Philosophy and Religion*. New Jersey: Humanities Press.

Robbins, Peter. 1982. *The British Hegelians: 1875–1925*. New York and London: Garland Publishing, Inc.

Saxonhouse, Arlene W. 1993. "Texts and Canons: The Status of the 'Great Books' in Political Theory. In *Political Science: The State of the Discipline II*. Edited by Ada W. Finifter. Washington: American Political Science Association.

Sexton, Steve. 2003. "UC Looks to Suspend Policy Precluding Politics in Classroom". *Washington Times*, 7 March, final edition. A6.

Shapiro, Ian. 2002. "Problems, Methods, and Theories in the Study of Politics, or What's Wrong with Political Science and What to Do About It". *Political Theory* 30(4):596–619.

Skinner, Quentin. 1988. "A Reply to My Critics". In *Meaning and Context: Quentin Skinner and his Critics*. Edited and introduced by James Tully. Princeton: Princeton University Press. 231–288.

— [1969] 1988. "Meaning and Understanding in the History of Ideas". Reprinted in *Meaning and Context: Quentin Skinner and his Critics*. Edited and introduced by James Tully. Princeton:

Princeton University Press. Originally published in *History and Theory* 8:3–53.

— [1972] 1988. "'Social Meaning' and the Explanation of Social Action". Reprinted in *Meaning and Context: Quentin Skinner and his Critics*. Edited and introduced by James Tully. Princeton: Princeton University Press. Originally published in *Philosophy, Politics and Society*, series IV. Edited by Peter Laslett, W.G. Runciman and Quentin Skinner. Oxford: Basil Blackwell. 136–57.

— [1974] 1988. "Some Problems in the Analysis of Political Thought and Action". Reprinted in *Meaning and Context: Quentin Skinner and his Critics*. Edited and introduced by James Tully. Princeton: Princeton University Press. Originally published in *Political Theory* 23:277–303.

— [1976] 1988. "Motives, Intentions and the Interpretation of Texts". Reprinted in *Meaning and Context: Quentin Skinner and his Critics*. Edited and introduced by James Tully. Princeton: Princeton University Press. Originally published in *On Literary Intention*. Edited by D. Newton de Molina. Edinburgh: Edinburgh University Press. 210–21.

— [1980] 1988. "Language and Social Change". Revised and Reprinted in *Meaning and Context: Quentin Skinner and his Critics*. Edited and introduced by James Tully. Princeton: Princeton University Press. Originally published in *The State of Language*. Edited L. Michaels and C. Ricks. Berkeley: University of California Press. 562–78.

Snell, Bruno. 1953. *The Discovery of the Mind: The Greek Origins of European Thought*. Translated by T.G. Rosenmeyer. Cambridge, MA: Harvard University Press.

Stewart, J.A. 1892. *Notes on the Nicomachean Ethics of Aristotle*. Vol. 1. Oxford: Clarendon Press.

1909. *Plato's Doctrine of Ideas*. Oxford: Clarendon Press.

Strauss, Leo. 1950. *Natural Right and History*. Chicago and London: University of Chicago Press.

— 1989. *An Introduction to Political Philosophy: Ten Essays by Leo Strauss*. Edited by Hilail Gildin. Detroit: Wayne State University Press.

Taylor, A.E. 1963. *Platonism and Its Influence*. New York: Cooper Square Publishers, Inc.

— 1969. *Aristotle on His Predecessors*. Second Edition. La Salle, IL: Open Court Publishing Co.

Thucydides. 1982. *The Peloponnesian War*. Translated by Richard Crawley. Revised by T.E. Wick. New York: The Modern Library.

— 1998. *The Peloponnesian War*. Translated by Steven Lattimore. Indianapolis and Cambridge: Hackett Publishing Company, Inc.

Tully, James. 2002. "Political Philosophy as Critical Activity". *Political Theory* 30(4):533–555.

Vincent, Andrew and Raymond Plant. 1984. *Philosophy, Politics and Citizenship: The Life and Thought of the British Idealists.* Oxford: Basil Blackwell.

Zeller, Eduard. 1868. *Socrates and the Socratic Schools.* Trans. Oswald J. Reichel. London: Longmans, Green, & Co.

— 1881. *A History of Greek Philosophy From the Earliest Period to the Time of Socrates.* Translated by S.F. Alleyne. 2 Volumes. Longmans, Green and Co. Volume II: "The Pre-Socratic Philosophy".

— 1962. *Plato and the Older Academy.* Translated by Sarah Francis Alleyne and Alfred Goodwin. New York: Russell and Russell, Inc.

Zuckert, Catherine H. 1996. *Postmodern Platos: Nietzsche, Heidegger, Gadamer, Strauss, Derrida.* Chicago and London: University of Chicago Press.

INDEX

A

Anaxagoras, 17, 18, 37, 39-40, 60
Anaximander, 12, 26-28
Anaximenes, 27, 33
anti-foundationalism, 9
Apology, 62, 76
aporia, 74
arche, 25
Arendt, Hannah, 1n1, 6, 134n22
Aristotle
  early study of, 9
  and education, 56
  and experience, 70, 73
  Ethics, 2, 70
  and happiness, 73
  method of, 123-124
  and necessary goods, 71
  and philosophy, 38-39
  on Plato's Forms, 80
  Politics, 2
  on his predecessors, 39-40
atomism, 37
Austin, J.L., 125, 128n18
authority (political), 23
Ayer, A.J., 19n5

B

Barker, Ernest, 38
Bentham, Jeremy, 47
Berkeley, 20
Bloom, Allan, 73n5
Bosanquet, Bernard, 7, 70n4, 91, 100n17
Bradley, F.H., 4n2, 9, 18, 93, 93n6, 95n7, 99
British idealism, 5
Burke, Edmund, 12, 113
Burnet, John
  biographical data, 20
  Oakeshott's use of, 19
Bush, George W., 115, 116, 119, 121

C

Cavarero, Adriana, 134n22
Cephalus, 13, 66, 69-75, 87, 139, 142
Cicero, 73
Coats, Wendell John, 5, 61n15
Coleridge, 60
Collingwood, R.G., 138n1, 139
concepts, 122-124
concrete universal, 27, 92, 131n20
context of political utterances, 118-120, 118n8
conversation, 15, 140, 141-143
Cudworth, 18, 58-59

D

Dahl, Robert, 120, 121, 127
Democritus, 38
Dewey, John, 124n14

E

education, 14, 15, 44-45 (in Greece), 56, 57, 61, 140
Empedokles, 37-38, 39n19
Encyclopaedists, 48
Epicureanism, 24
Erdmann, Johann, 20, 20n7
experiential unity, 12
explanatory thinking
  in general principles, 116-117
  and philosophy, 117-119

F

Ferrier, James Frederick
  biographical data, 20
  and Hegel, 20n6
  Oakeshott's use of, 19
  and philosophy, v, 26, 28-30, 34
Forester, E.M., 6n4
Franco, Paul, 4n2, 10n8, 61n15, 135n23